ISO 22301:2019 and Business Continuity Management

Understand how to plan, implement and enhance a business continuity management system (BCMS)

ISO 22301:2019 and Business Continuity Management

Understand how to plan, implement and enhance a business continuity management system (BCMS)

ALAN CALDER

IT Governance Publishing

IT Governance Publishing Ltd
Unit 3, Clive Court
Bartholomew's Walk
Cambridgeshire Business Park
Ely, Cambridgeshire
CB7 4EA
United Kingdom
www.itgovernancepublishing.co.uk

First edition published in the United Kingdom in 2021 by IT Governance Publishing

ISBN 978-1-78778-299-0

ABOUT THE AUTHOR

Alan Calder founded IT Governance Limited in 2002 and began working full time for the company in 2007. He is now Group CEO of GRC International Group plc, the AIM-listed company that owns IT Governance Ltd. Prior to this, Alan had a number of roles including CEO of Business Link London City Partners from 1995 to 1998 (a government agency focused on helping growing businesses to develop), CEO of Focus Central London from 1998 to 2001 (a training and enterprise council), CEO of Wide Learning from 2001 to 2003 (a supplier of e-learning) and the Outsourced Training Company (2005). Alan was also chairman of CEME (a public private sector skills partnership) from 2006 to 2011.

Alan is an acknowledged international cyber security guru and a leading author on information security and IT governance issues. He has been involved in the development of a wide range of information security management training courses that have been accredited by the International Board for IT Governance Qualifications (IBITGQ). Alan has consulted for clients in the UK and abroad, and is a regular media commentator and speaker.

CONTENTS

INTRODUCTION

In an increasingly volatile world – exemplified by the COVID-19 pandemic – organisations are looking at business continuity with new eyes. The illusion of business as a rampart against which the waves of the world break harmlessly has been shattered; it is no longer possible to pretend that an organisation can weather all storms equally, or that the limited contingencies organisations develop are sufficient to protect them against the rapidly changing face of modern risk.

Business continuity – the discipline of planning for, protecting against and ensuring recovery from disruptive events – is more important than it has ever been. As a result, more and more organisations are looking to ISO 22301 – the international standard that defines the requirements for a business continuity management system (BCMS) – to safeguard their future.

This book walks you through the requirements of ISO 22301:2019, explaining what they mean and how your organisation can achieve compliance in a practical manner. Whether you are seeking certification against the Standard or are simply looking to benefit from business continuity concepts and practices without developing a formal system, this book contains all you need to know.

The road to business continuity

The genesis of business continuity management (BCM) as a formal discipline arguably lies in the introduction of computers to business. The considerable benefits derived from the use of computers in speeding up business processes and improving productivity soon became dulled by the realisation that, like any machine, computers could malfunction or fail, resulting in significant disruption.

Sensing a gap in the market, computer manufacturers (and eventually, dedicated service providers) began to offer 'disaster recovery' services to help organisations restore their computer systems in the event of failure. These early offerings were the beginning of business continuity as we know it today.

Over time, disaster recovery evolved from a solely technological consideration to one encompassing the entire organisation, culminating in the publication of early business continuity standards such as PAS 56: 2003 (Guide to business continuity management). The arrival of BS 25999-1 in 2006 and BS 25999-2 in 2007 defined a formal approach for UK organisations engaged in anything to do with business continuity or resilience, and the possibility of national accreditation for those looking to set themselves apart from their competitors.

As worldwide demand for a business continuity standard grew, the International Organization for Standardization (ISO) developed a new business continuity standard, based in part on the earlier standards, which was published in 2012. ISO 22301:2012 *Societal security – Business continuity management systems – Requirements* described the specification for a BCMS – a formal methodology that organisations could use to prepare for and respond effectively to disruptive events.

As an ISO standard, ISO 22301 offered benefits over older standards. It was developed to match the movement towards a common structure for management system standards, allowing it to integrate easily with other management systems and streamlining adoption by experienced management system practitioners. It also offered the opportunity to achieve internationally recognised certification – a valuable mark of assurance in an increasingly insecure age and a significant advance over the limited national accreditation available for BS 25999.

October 2019 saw the release of ISO 22301:2019 *Security and resilience — Business continuity management systems — Requirements*. Although largely an administrative revision, the new standard retains all the benefits of the 2012 edition, but uses clearer language and clarifies several key concepts, making the process of implementing a BCMS easier and more accessible.

A note on business interruption insurance

One of the more common arguments against implementing a BCMS is that the organisation has business interruption insurance, and therefore a BCMS is not necessary. Business interruption insurance compensates organisations for profit loss during the indemnity period, which can range from a few weeks or months to several years.

However, business interruption insurance does not compensate for losses that occur outside the indemnity period, or for loss of future business that follows a disruption. Most such insurance is designed with physical disruptions in mind – fire, flood, etc. – and offers little or no cover for disruptions that do not arise from a physical event. Many organisations discovered this to their detriment after claims related to the COVID-19 pandemic were rejected by insurers.[1] In the rare cases where such cover is offered, it comes at a significant premium.

As a reactive rather than proactive measure, insurance provides minimal defence against disruption – all it can do is mitigate the financial impact. If a disruption lasts longer than the indemnity period, or if the disruption experienced is excluded by the terms and conditions, then the overall benefit of the insurance diminishes rapidly.

Even if you have the most comprehensive policy available, you must still find a way to mitigate the effects of the disruption while it is occurring and return to business as usual once it has ended. Insurance should be considered complementary to business continuity, but it cannot replace a BCMS, and insurance alone is not a defence.

---

[1] Mary Williams Walsh, "Businesses Thought They Were Covered for the Pandemic. Insurers Say No.", *The New York Times*, August 2020, www.nytimes.com/2020/08/05/business/business-interruption-insurance-pandemic.html.

CHAPTER 1: USING ISO 22301

Readers approaching ISO 22301 for the first time can be forgiven for feeling some trepidation on sitting down to read it. Business continuity is far from the most accessible discipline, and the terminology and processes used can be complex and opaque, especially for new practitioners.

Fortunately, the order in which the Standard is written is, by and large, the order in which the BCMS should be implemented, so it is perfectly feasible to begin at the start and implement each requirement in turn. Although you can implement some requirements in an order other than that specified in the Standard, some aspects of the BCMS can only be effectively implemented after others are in place. It would be challenging to develop a comprehensive internal audit programme, for example, if large chunks of the BCMS are not yet implemented – the internal audit requirements are placed towards the end of the Standard for that reason.

The PDCA cycle

ISO 22301 applies the Plan-Do-Check-Act (PDCA) cycle to both implement and maintain the BCMS. PDCA was developed by quality management pioneer Walter Shewhart in the decades following World War Two, and has since become the core improvement philosophy behind many management system standards.[2] The PDCA cycle is an iterative approach to improvement that should be applied to any action taken in respect of the BCMS.

The PDCA cycle is as straightforward as it sounds. Before taking any action, plan out how it should proceed (plan). Once your planning is complete, take the action in accordance with the plan (do). Once the action has been implemented, monitor and evaluate its effectiveness (check), then use the information gained to make improvements (act).

Each iteration of the cycle improves your knowledge of the system, and ensures that change is applied in a controlled manner. Applying PDCA whenever changes are made to the BCMS should ensure that any change that introduces a detrimental effect is quickly identified and mitigated.

It may sound onerous to apply PDCA to every single action taken in respect of the management system, but it is important to remember that the planning and level of analysis should be proportionate to the action concerned. There is no need to create extensive plans and in-depth analyses of relatively minor actions, but more complex actions, or those that could result in potentially serious impacts, should be subject to more detailed consideration.

The Standard does not require evidence that you are applying PDCA, so there is no need to document the planning and analysis for every single action, and the topic is unlikely to arise in any detail during audits unless there is evidence that

---

[2] Although developed by Shewhart, PDCA was popularised by W. Edwards Deming (another key figure in the development of quality management systems). Deming preferred 'plan-do-*study*-act' in the later years of his career, as it emphasises the need for analysis and evaluation of the action, rather than simple inspection, as implied by 'check'.

actions are frequently taken without considering their potential impact. That said, it is useful to retain some evidence of the application of PDCA when preparing for initial certification, and more generally, for complex or high-risk actions taken within a mature BCMS, in case a third-party auditor questions your approach.

Companion standards

Like many management system standards, ISO 22301 is supported by companion standards that expand on specific aspects of the management system, or offer guidance on applying the requirements in the 'parent' standard.

ISO 22301 is supported by two such standards:

1. ISO 22313:2020 (*Security and resilience — Business continuity management systems — Guidance on the use of ISO 22301*); and
2. ISO/TS 22317:2015 (*Societal security — Business continuity management systems — Guidelines for business impact analysis*).

The former offers general guidance on the application of ISO 22301, and the latter provides detailed guidance on the methodology behind business impact analysis (BIA; a key part of any BCMS).

Unlike many supporting standards, which frequently add little to further the reader's understanding of the topic at hand, ISO 22313 and ISO/TS 22317 both expand on the requirements of ISO 22301 in a detailed and useful manner. They are an excellent resource for any organisation looking to implement a BCMS.

Integrated management systems

Many organisations already operate a management system, such as ISO 9001 (quality management), ISO 27001 (information security management) or ISO 14001 (environmental management).

All ISO management systems, including ISO 22301, can be combined with any other ISO management system to create an integrated management system (IMS). This provides several advantages: common functions such as internal audit and management review can be adapted to cover the requirements of multiple management systems with only minor impact on resources, while the context of the organisation, interested parties and other common factors will already have been identified to a great extent, saving time.

An integrated approach results in an IMS that makes the most efficient use of resources to achieve the goals of the constituent management systems. Not only does this make for a robust assurance framework, but it can also form the basis for a strong culture of governance and improvement that benefits the entire organisation.

'Shall' and 'should'

As you read through the Standard, there are two important terms to watch out for: 'shall' and 'should'. Any instance of 'shall' refers to a mandatory requirement of the Standard – something that must be present for the BCMS to be considered in conformity with ISO 22301. Auditors will expect you to be able to show evidence that a 'shall' requirement has been implemented.

'Should' refers to a recommendation – something that could benefit the organisation or the BCMS, but which is not a mandatory requirement (and for which you will not be expected to provide evidence). You will also encounter 'may' and 'can', both of which refer to permissions or possibilities that can be deployed if they suit the organisation.

'Top management'

All ISO management system standards refer to senior leaders as 'top management'. Top management refers to the board, executive leadership team or other top-level authority responsible for the organisation, and this book will also use this term.

In particular, 'top management' refers to those ultimately responsible for the organisation, or part of an organisation that operates the BCMS. For example, in the case of an organisation that operates multiple sites under a single, overarching BCMS, top management are the persons responsible for overseeing all those sites. If the same multi-site organisation were to operate a separate BCMS at each individual site, then top management would refer to the persons responsible for the site in question.

CHAPTER 2: CONTEXT, INTERESTED PARTIES AND SCOPE

4.1 Context of the organisation

Before implementing any management system, it is necessary to identify the context in which the organisation operates, and any issues that arise from it that might affect the organisation or its BCMS.

Organisations implementing their first management system sometimes struggle with this requirement. The Standard does not provide much information on what this process should look like or what its outputs should be, and as a result, even experienced practitioners approach this requirement in radically different ways.

The goal of this requirement is not merely to reiterate the obvious – organisation X is in the business of Y, and so on – instead, the requirement drives analysis of the conditions (both internal and external) that the organisation operates within to ensure that those conditions do not adversely affect the organisation or its BCMS. By considering where you are now, and where you are likely to be in the future, you lay the foundations for effective governance.

'Internal issues' can include the products or services the organisation offers (including any standards, e.g. safety standards, that they must adhere to), employees and unions, the culture and values of the organisation, operational and development priorities, warranty and service requirements, governance concerns (such as any other management systems already in operation) and more.

'External issues' can include legal and regulatory requirements (whether they apply to the products or services offered or to the organisation itself), the supply chain, media and communication, the environment in which the organisation operates (whether financial, operational, etc.) and even technological changes in the field that might affect your business, such as a competitor developing a superior product or a new method of manufacturing that reduces cost.

It is important to note that the process of identifying context should not focus solely on issues that might result in a negative impact. You should also consider opportunities that could lead to a positive outcome, as these can have just as significant an effect (albeit in a different way) on the organisation and its BCMS.

One method to define the external context of the organisation (though by no means the only method) is to perform a 'PESTLE' analysis. This approach places external issues into six categories;

1. **Political**;
2. **Economic**;
3. **Social**;
4. **Technological**;
5. **Legal**; and
6. **Environmental**.

This provides an at-a-glance view of the issues affecting your organisation. At this stage, you are not trying to identify specific risks that may arise from the issues you identify; this is a macro-scale exercise designed to capture sources of potential impact, not the impacts themselves.

Internal context can be identified through a 'SWOT' analysis. This method considers the organisation's strengths, weaknesses, opportunities and threats, and is often used in tandem with a PESTLE analysis. The combination of the two makes for a wide-ranging view of the organisation, which satisfies the requirements of the Standard.

The Standard does not require you to retain evidence that you have considered the context of the organisation, but the external and internal context outputs feed directly into the requirement to address risks and opportunities related to the BCMS in part six of the Standard, so it is important to keep a record of those outputs for use in that procedure. You will also need to periodically review and update the issues you have recorded as part of the BCMS improvement process, which is a lot easier to do if they are documented.

4.2 Interested parties

Once you have identified the context your organisation operates in, the next step is to identify 'interested parties' and their requirements.

Interested parties refers to stakeholders of any sort, those to whom your organisation owes a duty of care (whether inside or outside the organisation) and those that could affect, or be affected by, the BCMS. The list of potential interested parties is long, and can include:

- Customers;
- Suppliers and distributors;
- Shareholders and investors;
- Regulators and enforcement bodies;
- Employees and contractors;
- Media; and

- Neighbours, organisations that share the premises, members of the public, etc.

Each interested party has its own requirements. Your suppliers, for example, will no doubt require that you pay their invoices on time, while regulators will require that you follow applicable laws, contact authorities when appropriate, etc. Interested parties may have multiple requirements; if this is the case, you should identify those that are relevant to your organisation. As with the context of the organisation, this is a macro-scale exercise intended to identify the parties and their requirements, not the risks or opportunities that might arise from those requirements.

The outputs from this procedure feed directly into the requirements in part six of the Standard, and you will be required to review and update them periodically. Therefore, although not explicitly required, you should keep a record of the parties and their requirements to demonstrate the link between the two, and to assist with the review process.

4.2.2 Legal and regulatory requirements

Section 4.4.2 of the Standard requires that you identify, document and assess applicable legal requirements that are related to the continuity of your products or services, or to the resources and activities involved in delivering them, and ensure that they are considered when implementing and maintaining your BCMS.

If you provide digital services in the EU or UK, for example, you may be in scope of the EU Directive on security of network and information systems (the NIS Directive; or the NIS Regulations in the UK), which requires specific continuity measures depending on the service provided.[3] Similarly, US healthcare providers in scope of the Health Insurance Portability and Accountability Act (HIPAA) must develop a disaster recovery plan and ensure it is tested.[4]

Many organisations already operate a register of legal requirements. If you do not, you will need to create one. A spreadsheet or similar document is perfectly sufficient.

ISO 22301 requires that you keep the register (or whatever method you use to document your legal requirements) up to date. An annual or twice-annual review will be adequate to ensure that the register is properly maintained, though the person responsible for maintaining it should also be expected to keep a weather eye on the news, relevant industry publications or other media that might provide advance notice of upcoming changes to relevant laws.

4.3 Scope of the BCMS

Before implementing a BCMS, you first need to define the system boundaries – what it will include, and what it will exclude. The scope of the BCMS is a key part of the initial implementation exercise, and should be considered carefully, as it will strongly influence the certification process.

---

[3] EU Directive on security of network and information systems, Article 16, *https://ec.europa.eu/digital-single-market/en/network-and-information-security-nis-directive*.

[4] US Health Insurance Portability and Accountability Act, 45 CFR § 164.308, *www.ecfr.gov/cgi-bin/retrieveECFR?gp=&SID=dc2f5801ea0b945b804f0918ce08c7db&mc=true&n=pt45.1.164&r=PART&ty=HTML#se45.2.164_1308*.

For smaller organisations operating at a single site, the scope will likely cover the whole organisation, while larger organisations may operate one overarching BCMS that covers all sites, or multiple site-specific ones. When determining the scope of your BCMS, consider the following:

- Products and/or services
- Countries or regions of operation, and individual sites or buildings
- Organisational divisions, e.g. the constituent organisations within a larger group
- Operational divisions, e.g. the different departments, etc. at a single site

The Standard also requires that you consider the context of the organisation and the requirements of interested parties, and the goals and obligations your organisation is subject to, during this process. In practice, this means accounting for legal requirements, the expectations of interested parties that are directly relevant, such as customers, suppliers and regulatory authorities, and any obligations in respect of the services your organisation offers. If your contracts stipulate that you will provide 24/7 warranty support, for example, it makes little sense to exclude your service department from the scope of the BCMS.

All dependencies on which the operations within scope rely, such as materials or resources, are considered in scope by default – after all, without them, achieving continuity would not be possible. You do not need to identify every dependency at this stage, but an awareness of the more significant dependencies is beneficial, in that it may reveal other functions of the business that rely on the same dependencies in less visible ways (and therefore may need to be included in the scope).

The scope does not necessarily have to cover the entire organisation. Some organisations may not need to recover all products or services in order to continue operating, while large organisations with multiple locations might restrict the scope to a single critical site. Although exclusions are permitted, any exclusion you make must not affect your ability to ensure continuity, as determined by the risk assessment and BIA processes defined later in the Standard.

Your rationale for any exclusion should be sound and documented in detail, as the auditor will ask you to explain it during the certification process, to confirm that the exclusion will not affect your continuity capabilities. The auditor may challenge the explanation and, if not satisfied, they may ask that you reconsider the exclusion.

The scope must be recorded and maintained as documented information. Most organisations take one of two routes in this respect:

1. A standalone scope statement; or
2. Inclusion of the scope in the BCMS policy statement.

Neither option is superior, though more complex scopes naturally lend themselves to a standalone statement.

Once you have achieved certification, you should review the scope of the BCMS during each management review (see chapter 9) to ensure that it continues to account for all necessary aspects of the organisation. The scope will also be a discussion topic during each surveillance audit, for the same reason.

4.4 BCMS

This clause requires that you implement a BCMS, and the necessary processes to support it, in accordance with the requirements of the Standard. Although it may seem somewhat superfluous, the purpose of the clause is to emphasise the need to implement and maintain the processes and interactions that support the operation of the BCMS.

All management systems (and all business operations more generally) rely on processes to function. It is therefore always in the best interests of the organisation that its processes are clear, practical, well documented and kept up to date. This smacks of stating the obvious, yet for many organisations, processes remain an afterthought. All too often, auditors encounter processes that are out of date and poorly maintained – covered in handwritten amendments, lacking version control, missing sections or entire pages. Unfortunately, this is usually an indication that the organisation does not take the management system very seriously.

Poorly controlled processes place the operations they support – and by extension, the BCMS and the wider organisation – at risk. Effective process control is a key requirement of any management system, and both certification and surveillance audits will involve a review of the processes that are pertinent to the parts of the BCMS the auditor is examining. If the auditor finds that a process in use is out of date, for example, they may require you to make corrections, and look deeper into areas that might contain similar examples of poor maintenance.

The Standard does not require a specific format or method for the development of processes, and neither does this book. Every organisation develops and documents processes in its own way and there is little need for additional guidance on the subject. However, if you do not have experience in process or documentation design, toolkits containing template documents and processes are commercially available, and can save you a significant amount of time.[5]

---

[5] For example, the ISO 22301 BCMS Toolkit, available from IT Governance: *www.itgovernance.co.uk/shop/product/iso-22301-bcms-toolkit*.

CHAPTER 3: LEADERSHIP, POLICY AND RESPONSIBILITIES

5.1 Leadership and commitment

As with any major business project, no BCMS implementation project will be successful without commitment and support from top management.

Historically, the bulk of the responsibility for the implementation and operation of management systems fell to the management representative (i.e. a quality manager, business continuity manager, etc.), with top management's hands-on involvement largely limited to the management review (see chapter 9). In 2012, however, this changed.

The introduction of Annex SL created a common high-level structure that all ISO management system standards must adhere to. This common structure standardised some aspects that are common to all management systems, such as management review, internal audit and leadership responsibilities. The changes to leadership responsibilities caused a minor stir, as they require top management to be more directly involved in the management systems operated by their organisation, instead of delegating their responsibilities to a representative.

Demonstrating leadership

Clause 5.1 contains a list of requirements that apply to top management, none of which are particularly surprising or controversial. Some of them can be delegated in the traditional manner, such as providing resources for the BCMS or integrating the BCMS into the organisation's processes, or should occur naturally, such as the requirement to support other managerial roles. Proof that these requirements are being met should be largely self-evident; it will be clear to an auditor whether the BCMS is appropriately resourced and integrated, for example, with only minimal investigation.

The other requirements pose a more complex problem, as top management must be directly involved in their delivery. Communicating the importance of continuity and of complying with the BCMS, for example, might be demonstrated by an all-staff briefing hosted by top management, while promoting continual improvement might be demonstrated by effective management reviews and regular communication regarding the nonconformity process. Of course, in order to comply with any of these requirements, top management will need to have a good understanding of business continuity and the BCMS, so training may be necessary.

Although the Standard does not require that the outputs of these activities (with the exception of the policy and objectives) are maintained as documented information, you will still need some evidence to demonstrate that these activities took place and that top management took part. Such evidence might take several forms:

- Meeting minutes;
- Records of BCMS awareness or training sessions;
- Communications regarding the BCMS and its requirements, etc.

Auditors will approach these requirements in different ways – for some, detailed interviews with top management will be sufficient, while others will want to see more concrete evidence – so you should be as prepared as possible, especially when you are approaching your initial certification audit.

Another challenge arises in respect of internal audit. Auditing top management's compliance with the requirements can be intimidating and auditors must approach those audits, and any potential nonconformities, with care. If possible, internal audits of the leadership requirements should be carried out by a senior member of the auditing team.

Whether internal or external, top management will need to make themselves available for audits. Certification and surveillance audits are often scheduled months in advance, but internal audits will need to be planned effectively to ensure top management are available.

5.2 Policy

The business continuity policy is one of the most important documents in the BCMS. The policy acts as a statement of intent and commitment for the BCMS, and defines your organisation's approach to continuity in broad terms. It will be shared with stakeholders inside and outside the organisation and should therefore be as concise and clear as possible while still meeting requirements.

The Standard defines several requirements for the policy, the first of which is easily missed – top management must be the ones to establish it. Ideally, they should be involved in drafting the policy, as they will have the widest understanding of the organisation, the field it operates in, the various legal requirements that may apply and the scope and intent of the BCMS. They should also be the ones to announce the policy to the wider organisation, both to emphasise how important it is to comply with the policy and the BCMS, and to demonstrate top management's support for the overall programme.

Although not strictly required by ISO 22301, it is sensible to retain a record of the policy drafting process (e.g. meeting minutes) when approaching initial certification, in case it is necessary to demonstrate top management's involvement in the process.

The policy must:

- Be appropriate for the organisation;
- Provide a framework for setting business continuity objectives;
- Include a commitment to satisfy applicable requirements; and
- Include a commitment to continually improve the BCMS.

The first requirement simply means that you must develop the policy to suit your organisation. Although this seems like stating the obvious, a surprising number of organisations simply try to copy or modify a policy from another organisation. If your policy does not fully account for your organisation's culture, mode of operation, etc., it is unlikely to be very effective.

The framework for setting business continuity objectives is an area where some organisations struggle, since the statement itself is not very clear. What this means is that the policy must broadly define the aspects for which business continuity objectives will be set, and this is usually achieved in the body of the policy text rather than as a separate list.

Statements such as 'Organisation X is committed to ensuring the effectiveness of the BCMS' can be linked directly to BCMS effectiveness objectives (e.g. reduction in the number of nonconformities issued), while 'Organisation X will work to reduce the recovery time of [prioritised activities]' can be linked to continual improvement objectives such as progressive reductions in recovery times. It is not necessary to include the objectives themselves in the body of the policy – all you need to demonstrate is that there is a link between the policy wording and your objectives.

Some organisations choose to include the scope of the BCMS and BC objectives in the policy, while others do not. Although ISO 22313 does recommend that the policy specify the scope, it is not a mandatory requirement, and nothing in ISO 22301 or 22313 suggests that you should define your BC objectives in the policy itself.

The last two policy requirements are relatively straightforward:

1. The policy must contain commitments to satisfy applicable requirements; and
2. To continually improve the BCMS.

These need only be simple statements, such as 'Organisation X is committed to compliance with all applicable legal, contractual and other requirements', and 'Organisation X is committed to the continual improvement of the BCMS'. Of course, the statements must be backed up by actions, but for the purposes of the policy document, the statements are enough to meet the requirements.

Communicating the policy

The Standard also includes requirements for documenting and communicating the business continuity policy. It must be retained as documented information (see chapter 5), and you must communicate it inside the organisation and to interested parties as appropriate.

Communicating the policy inside the organisation can be done in a variety of ways, including email and more involved methods such as all-company briefings. Auditors will check compliance with this requirement either by asking for evidence that the communication took place, or (more likely) by interviewing staff members and asking them if they know what the policy is and where to find it. You should ensure that all staff know how to locate the policy at a minimum.

Communicating the policy outside of the organisation often takes place via the company website, though it is beneficial to keep a copy in a protected document format (e.g. pdf) so it can be provided to interested parties on request.

5.3 Roles, responsibilities and authorities

In any major implementation project, someone must be responsible for overseeing the project and ensuring it proceeds as planned. ISO 22301 contains three separate requirements in this respect.

Firstly, top management must ensure that responsibilities and authorities for the various roles involved in the BCMS (auditors, crisis management teams, etc.) are assigned and communicated. Although the assignment of such roles will probably occur naturally as the project progresses, you should consider how you might provide evidence that they were communicated – e.g. records of a company briefing or an intranet page listing key personnel. You should also consider including BCMS responsibilities in job descriptions and contracts for relevant staff members.

The other two requirements are to assign responsibility for:

1. Ensuring the BCMS meets the requirements of the Standard; and
2. Reporting on the performance of the BCMS to top management.

How this is achieved will depend on the size and nature of the organisation. Small and medium-sized organisations operating from a single site may find it sufficient to hire or designate a single manager who is accountable for the BCMS and its operation – usually referred to as a business continuity manager. Alternatively, they may choose to fold the role into an existing but similar one, such as a head of compliance, though care must be taken to ensure that the person concerned has the capacity to perform the new role alongside any existing duties, and that there are no conflicts of interest.

Larger organisations operating across multiple sites or as part of a wider corporate group will necessarily require a different approach. In such cases, it is common for each site to have a business continuity manager who is responsible for the BCMS and continuity operations specific to that site, while reporting to a higher authority (often a chief of operations or the board) overseeing business continuity throughout the group. This approach is the norm even in cases where the group operates a single, over-arching BCMS that applies to all its sites, as each site will inevitably require its own specific continuity plan and supporting operations.

Regardless of organisation size, the business continuity manager or equivalent, top-level role responsible for the

3: Leadership, policy and responsibilities

BCMS at a site should be a senior management role and should report directly to top management. Mid-level managers, department heads and similar roles often have strong opinions about how their department should be managed and may respond negatively to what they perceive as a role with less authority imposing conditions or actions. Ensuring that the top-level BCMS role is of at least equivalent authority goes a long way in minimising potential conflicts.

CHAPTER 4: PLANNING

6.1 Actions to address risks and opportunities

The first step in the implementation process is to identify the context of your organisation and the issues that arise from it, and the interested parties and their requirements. This part of the Standard uses those issues and requirements to identify and mitigate risks, and highlight opportunities that apply to the BCMS (risks related to business disruption are covered in a later section of ISO 22301).

The goal here, as stated in part 6.1.1 of the Standard, is to:

1. Provide assurance that the BCMS achieves its intended outcomes (i.e. that the organisation can recover from a disruption before the impact becomes unacceptable);
2. Reduce undesirable effects (i.e. eliminating factors that could impede or prevent the BCMS from achieving the intended outcomes); and
3. To achieve continual improvement (through application of PDCA, audits, etc.).

For each issue or requirement identified in your earlier work, consider how it might affect the BCMS. Legal requirements, for example, may require you to recover certain services within a set time frame. This is a risk to both the organisation and the BCMS – if not properly accounted for, the BCMS may not ensure recovery within the prescribed time frame, which could lead to fines or other punitive action. Health and safety requirements (an internal issue) might make it necessary to conduct recovery actions with specific protective equipment or in a certain order, raising risks around provision and availability of that equipment, and proper application of procedures in the event of a disruption.

Some issues and requirements can result in opportunities rather than risks. For example, if continuity measures are required by law, you could differentiate your organisation from competitors by going further than the minimum required and publicising your efforts. Although the number of risks will naturally be higher than the number of opportunities, in most cases, an exhaustive analysis will always highlight at least one opportunity. Failure to identify any at all will suggest to auditors that you have not carried out a strong enough analysis, so if you really cannot identify any, document the results so you have something to show an auditor.

Although there is no cast-iron requirement to document the risks and opportunities you identify, recording them alongside the issues and requirements of interested parties (e.g. in different tabs of the same spreadsheet) streamlines the next stage of the process, and serves as useful evidence to present to an auditor. However you choose to record them, the link between each issue or requirement and the risks or opportunities that arise from it should be as clear as possible.

6.1.2 Addressing risks and opportunities

Once you have identified the risks and opportunities, the next step is to take action to address them, as required by 6.1.2 of the Standard.

ISO 22301 does not expressly require that the risks and opportunities identified in 6.1.1 are subjected to risk assessment in the traditional sense, and traditional risk assessment may not always be appropriate for the kind of broad risks and opportunities that arise from issues of context and the requirements of interested parties. Instead, you can simply consider the possible effects on the BCMS (whether positive or negative) for each risk or opportunity, and how you will address them.

This is not to say that you cannot apply a detailed risk assessment process to these risks and opportunities if you prefer to. Whichever method you choose, you should have a clear idea of your organisation's risk tolerance – the level of risk you are prepared to accept before mitigating action is deemed necessary. With the kind of broad risks that generally arise out of the context of the organisation and the requirements of interested parties, top management are likely to have the best view of what is and is not tolerable.

There is also no explicit requirement to document the actions you take to address risks and opportunities – however, there are requirements to integrate the actions into your BCMS processes (by updating procedures, records, measurement methods, etc.) and to evaluate their effectiveness. Demonstrating the latter requirement without some documentation to describe the risk and the actions taken can be challenging, so if you have recorded the risks and opportunities in the same spreadsheet (etc.) that contains the issues and requirements, as advised earlier, it is sensible to record the actions taken, the chosen evaluation method, the outcome of the evaluations and any follow-up actions there as well.

This allows you to demonstrate a clear path from the initial identification of contextual issues and the requirements of interested parties, to the risks and opportunities that arise from them and the actions taken to address them, and finally to the evaluation of effectiveness and any further actions that arise from it. This approach will satisfy auditors at all stages of the certification process, and if properly maintained, will evolve into a useful record that shows how context and requirements, and their effect on the organisation, change over time.

6.2 Business continuity objectives and planning to achieve them

Business continuity objectives are both a driver of continual improvement and a means by which the overall effectiveness of the BCMS can be evaluated. All ISO management system standards contain a requirement to set objectives, and external auditors will review them at each surveillance audit, so it is important to get them right.

The Standard requires that business continuity objectives are consistent with the policy, measurable (where possible) and that they account for applicable requirements (legal, contractual, etc.). You must communicate your objectives to the wider organisation so that everyone is aware how their actions contribute to achieving them, and they must be monitored and updated as appropriate. From a practical perspective, objectives are unlikely to change very frequently (operating for several years with only minor adjustments to the same objectives is not uncommon), but significant changes to the way the organisation operates, corporate acquisitions or buyouts and similar notable events should provoke a review.

A popular and effective approach to defining objectives that meets all the requirements of the Standard is the 'SMART' method, which states that objectives should be specific, measurable, achievable, realistic and time bound. Examples of suitable objectives might include reducing overall recovery time, improving initial response times or preserving specific activities at a minimum level of operation (e.g. ensuring 80% of orders are shipped within two days). When defining an objective, you should also define how it will be measured – if you struggle to do this, then you should consider whether that objective is really suitable.

You will need to plan how you will achieve your objectives, including the necessary resources and responsibilities, target dates for completion and how you will evaluate the results of the actions you take to achieve them. Although the planning does not need to be maintained as documented information, external auditors will expect you to be able to show some evidence that planning has taken place and that it meets the requirements stated in 6.2.2 of ISO 22301, so consider retaining meeting minutes or documenting the evaluation process to use as evidence during an audit. You should also record the results of evaluations to better inform future objectives and identify improvement opportunities.

Objectives must be maintained as documented information. When defining objectives, remember that they must relate to business continuity in a direct way; if you have to go to great lengths to explain why a given objective is relevant to business continuity, it is unlikely to be appropriate. Likewise, in some organisations, there will be a natural urge on the part of some managers to skew objectives in directions they are more familiar with. 'Improving value for shareholders' may be a worthy goal in and of itself, but it has nothing to do with business continuity and is therefore unsuitable.

6.3 Planning changes to the BCMS

Most organisations are familiar with change management in one form or another – the process of planning, managing and evaluating changes to business systems to ensure that they deliver what is expected. ISO 22301 makes the management of changes to the BCMS an explicit requirement, though only in a relatively informal sense.

The Standard requires that you consider four common-sense aspects when planning changes to the BCMS:

1. What the changes are and what they are intended to achieve.
2. The integrity of the BCMS as a functioning system.
3. The availability of resources to carry out the change.
4. The allocation (or reallocation) of appropriate roles and responsibilities.

Perhaps the most important of these aspects is the integrity of the BCMS – how it operates as a functional system, and how the proposed changes will affect that system and, in turn, the continuity plans that arise from it. Even small changes can have unintended consequences that may not be immediately apparent, and those consequences have a nasty habit of taking effect at the worst possible time.

If your organisation already operates a change management system, you may be used to a much wider scope of consideration and planning, and a much more detailed process than the Standard requires. It is perfectly acceptable to route proposed changes to the BCMS through your existing change management system (provided the four requirements are accounted for), rather than develop a separate system solely for the BCMS.

If you do not operate a change management system, then it may be worth considering this requirement as a prompt to develop a formal process across the wider business. Such a system can have notable benefits beyond its application to the BCMS and can be applied to almost any example of business change, large or small, to ensure that changes are managed consistently and in an effective manner. The PDCA cycle provides an excellent base for such a process, should you choose to go down this route. It does not need to be extremely complex, but if you do implement one, you should record the results to inform future changes and improve overall risk management.

Although implementing formal change management is considered best practice, the Standard does not mandate that you develop a formal process – it simply asks that change is planned and managed (though without a formal process, it is difficult to make sure change is consistent and effective). There is no requirement to record the results of planning or even the outcome of the changes made, but as with all 'shall' requirements, being able to show some evidence, however small, that the requirements are met will go a long way in ensuring smooth audits.

CHAPTER 5: SUPPORT

7.1 Resources

It will come as no surprise that a BCMS, as with any other significant business project, requires resources both before and during implementation, and a commitment to maintain and improve it. Yet, all too often, management systems are hamstrung by a lack of appropriate resources, no doubt contributing to the horror stories of management system projects going off the rails and over-budget that are familiar to many senior leaders.

Top management are ultimately responsible for ensuring that sufficient resources are available for the project to succeed, and the Standard makes this clear in clause 5.1. It is therefore essential that top management are provided with the right information to make the necessary resources available. This will require a clear and comprehensive implementation plan, and associated budgets for both implementing and maintaining the BCMS over time.

The first resource consideration is people, both in the sense of ensuring sufficient staff and ensuring that they are competent to carry out BCMS-related roles. This is a common stumbling block, as organisations can be reluctant to invest in staff for a project they see as unproven, and in some cases may be prevented from hiring or training by parent organisations with tight grips on the purse-strings. Equally, it is common to see organisations place the various additional responsibilities for the BCMS onto existing staff with little consideration for the impact it will have on the performance of their normal duties and those related to the BCMS.

Unfortunately, if this occurs, there are few ways around it. However, if top management (and if necessary, any parent organisations) understand the value of the BCMS and are committed to it, such scenarios can be avoided.

The next resource consideration is equipment and facilities. In the event of a major fire or other source of widespread damage, a manufacturing organisation (for example) is unlikely to be able to access its facilities and the equipment therein. It will therefore be necessary to identify secondary locations, along with backup tools, safety gear and other equipment to ensure recovery proceeds as planned. For office-based organisations, the equipment and facilities that might be needed to ensure recovery will likely include office space, computers and the necessary infrastructure to operate and secure them, alongside more mundane items such as software licences, stationery, printers, etc.

This is not to say you must maintain a warehouse stocked with enough consumables to prepare for every eventuality – most common equipment requirements can be fulfilled by service providers at relatively short notice, whether it be computers and monitors or office stationery. Commercial Cloud systems in particular operate independently from your systems, and can be accessed from a home PC provided employees have secure logins (and defined policies on the use of their own devices).

Regardless of the nature of your organisation, you will need to ensure that you have copies of the processes and procedures that the organisation uses to operate (and ensure that they are kept up to date). You will need access to records, whether hard copy or electronic, of staff, customers, suppliers, etc., and contact information for relevant parties, along with the means to communicate with them (especially in respect of local or national authorities) during the disruption. If you have particular legal requirements (e.g. retaining backups for specified periods or ensuring a minimum level of service), you will need to ensure the resources you arrange are sufficient to ensure that you do not fall foul of the law.

The final resource is one likely to generate intense discussion and should be approached with care. Disruptions by their very nature imply some loss of revenue and increase in costs, both during the initial stage and throughout the recovery period, and although the BCMS and the continuity plan are designed to mitigate this as much as possible, it is unlikely that you will be able to return to 100% capacity immediately. To ensure that your organisation remains viable at the capacity level defined in the continuity plan (or longer, in extreme cases), it may be necessary to set aside 'buffer funding' to make up for any income shortfall.

7.2 Competence

Part 7.2 of the Standard places requirements on the competence of personnel whose work affects business continuity performance. This naturally includes those responsible for implementing and maintaining the BCMS and its outputs, and those who contribute to its success in a less direct manner.

You will first need to identify the skills, knowledge and/or experience required to perform the various roles and responsibilities within the BCMS. For example, those leading the project (including top management) must have a strong understanding of what a BCMS is and what it is intended to achieve, the specific requirements of ISO 22301, organisational and communication skills, and knowledge of risk assessment and risk management. Internal auditors will also need to understand the requirements of the Standard in detail and have the requisite auditing skills to perform their role.

All personnel with specific roles to play in a disruption should know how to locate the business continuity plan (BCP), the scenarios and triggers that will activate the plan, their own responsibilities and those of others and the wider chain of control and communication through which plans are activated and actions taken.

Those not immediately involved in the implementation or maintenance of the BCMS will still need to understand what the BCMS is, its intended purpose and the role they play in adhering to its requirements. The same may also apply to suppliers and other interested parties, depending on the nature of the organisation.

In some cases, the personnel involved will already have the requisite skills or experience. This is likely to be the case in respect of top management's organisational and communication skills, for example. The same is true if you are lucky enough to have an experienced business continuity practitioner within the organisation (provided their knowledge is current to the latest version of the Standard). Where this is the case, there is no need for additional training – simply define the experience necessary and record how the skills or experience of the person concerned meets the requirement.

Once you have identified any skill or knowledge gaps, on the other hand, you must then ensure that training or other methods are used to close them. For those directly involved in the BCMS and its implementation but who have not operated a BCMS (or any other kind of management system) before, training courses from reputable providers, such as IT Governance's Certified ISO 22301 BCMS Foundation, Lead Implementer and Lead Auditor training course, will play a key role.[6] Awareness programmes and staff briefings can be used to ensure that other personnel understand what is expected of them. You can also look to hire those with the necessary skills or experience.

In all cases where actions must be taken to ensure competence, the Standard requires that you evaluate the effectiveness of those actions. How you go about achieving this is up to you – you can, for example, provide questionnaires or short tests after training sessions, or evaluate a recent trainee's competence by examining the level of knowledge they display in an interview or discussion once the training is complete. Although you can evaluate the effectiveness of training by examining the success of the ongoing implementation, this is risky – if the training was not effective, time and money may be wasted reverting actions that are not beneficial to the implementation of the BCMS.

You must maintain "appropriate documented information as evidence of competence", and it will also be useful to retain evidence of the entire competence programme, from determining the necessary skills and experience, to the actions taken to achieve them and your evaluation of the effectiveness of those actions. Small to medium-sized organisations often develop a competency matrix – a spreadsheet containing the necessary skills, the actions taken and the results of evaluation, together with links to training

---

[6] All of IT Governance's ISO 22301 training courses can be found at *www.itgovernance.co.uk/iso22301-courses*.

certificates (or locations of hard copies) where appropriate. Larger organisations may use proprietary or purchased solutions for recording training requirements and outcomes, but ultimately, how you do it does not matter. Provided you can demonstrate to an auditor – and to yourself – a clear path from determination to provision, then to outcome and evaluation, you can be satisfied you have met the requirements of the Standard.

7.3 Awareness

For any management system to function, those working under its purview must understand what the system is and the role they play in ensuring it achieves its goals. ISO 22301 requires that all your employees (and any other workers under your control, such as contractors, temporary workers, etc.) are aware of the business continuity policy, how the work they do contributes to the success of the BCMS, the specific roles and responsibilities they have should a disruption occur and the potential consequences (e.g. disciplinary action) of not conforming to the BCMS's requirements.

The majority of organisations meet this requirement by deploying staff briefings and awareness training. This is often supplemented with written information on corporate intranets or shared file libraries, and by including awareness material in staff induction procedures to ensure that new employees understand the BCMS from the outset of their employment.

Briefings and awareness training sessions are usually short events (30 minutes or less) led by the project leader or business continuity manager, which cover the basics: what business continuity is, what the BCMS is, the continuity policy and what it means, what to expect during external and internal audits, and the broad strokes of how the business will respond to a disruption (e.g. moving to different premises, working from home, etc.) and what it will mean for affected employees.

Induction information is usually provided to new hires on a one-to-one basis alongside other common introductory information, such as health and safety or money-laundering requirements. Although there is no explicit requirement to provide information on business continuity during induction, failure to do so will likely prompt questions from auditors about the clear awareness gap from the employee's start date to the first awareness session they participate in.

Naturally, staff with more involved roles to play during or after a disruption will need more information. IT administrators and staff, facilities personnel and operational managers, for example, will all likely play key roles in responding to a disruption. Any such cases should be identified and resolved as part of your competence programme, though they should still participate in awareness sessions to ensure that their knowledge remains current. Awareness training should be repeated periodically for all employees, for the same reason – this is especially critical for a BCMS, as it may be a long time before a disruption arises, and large-scale testing of the plan, though it will occur, is unlikely to be a high-frequency event.

The Standard does not mandate that you keep records of awareness training as documented information. However, it makes sense to keep at least some records (e.g. date of awareness training, names of attendees, etc.) as an expansion of your competence programme. This will help you understand whether the awareness training is effective and help identify gaps that need filling.

External auditors will likely determine whether the awareness requirements have been met by interviewing employees and asking them if they know where the business continuity policy is, what it means to them, and generally probing their understanding of business continuity and the BCMS to see if their understanding is appropriate for their given role. That said, written evidence of awareness training that you can demonstrate during an audit will certainly not hurt.

7.4 Communication

The need to communicate internally and externally on matters of consequence will be familiar to all organisations, and the BCMS is certainly one such matter. Clause 7.4 of the Standard places requirements on the organisation to determine, in respect of the BCMS, the matters on which it deems communication necessary, who is responsible for communication, and when, how and to whom they will communicate.

It is important to note that this part of the Standard does not refer to the communications that are necessary in the event of a disruption – rather, it refers to those communications needed to ensure the BCMS operates as intended and achieves its goals, and to respond to the needs and expectations of interested parties.[7]

---

[7] Communication related to continuity plans and disruptions is covered in 8.4.3 of the Standard.

You will first need to determine the entities you need to communicate with, and what kind of communication is necessary. This will include informing staff of the BCMS and its goals, of any changes that occur throughout the lifecycle of the BCMS and how they affect staff and other interested parties, and the results of exercises, audits and improvements. Depending on the nature of the organisation, it may also include communication of requirements imposed on the BCMS by law or regulation, adherence to which is particularly critical. In some cases, it may be necessary to communicate with external parties such as regulators, or local or national authorities, either as a matter of course or in the event that certain defined thresholds are crossed – those thresholds will also need to be determined. Supplier communication will also no doubt be necessary in many cases.

Once this is done, you will need to decide who will communicate on the various matters you have deemed necessary. This will likely involve multiple parties, so the chain of communication and each person's responsibilities should be determined, and ideally, recorded. Consideration should also be given to the means and media through which the communications will occur. In practice, most communication is likely to be electronic, but there may still be occasions where other media is more appropriate – significant changes to the BCMS, for example, may be better communicated through informational posters in key areas, rather than a single email that could easily be forgotten amid the bustle of a busy working day.

As with the previous section, ISO 22301 does not mandate that you maintain records of, or procedures for, communication as documented information. Small and medium-sized organisations in which only a small number of people are responsible for communication can probably survive without a documented procedure, but the larger the organisation and the more personnel that are involved, the more benefit such a procedure will provide. For all sizes of organisation, records will prove beneficial too – not just in the sense of something you can use to demonstrate compliance during an audit, but also in identifying trends and patterns in communication that can be used to make improvements. If your organisation is subject to specific legal requirements in respect of business continuity, or must communicate with relevant authorities, then recording communications related to these is strongly recommended, even though the Standard does not require it.

7.5 Documented information

Every management system is built on documentation, and all management system standards use a specific term to describe documents that must be effectively controlled for the system to properly function. This term is 'documented information'.

Documented information falls into two categories, as per 7.5.1:

1. Those documents that the Standard defines as mandatory; and
2. Those documents that the organisation deems necessary to ensure the effectiveness of its BCMS.

Both must be controlled to the level defined in 7.5.2 and 7.5.3 (which we will consider shortly), so the key takeaway from 7.5.1 is that any document, process or record that falls outside the mandatory requirements, but is still necessary to ensure the proper operation of the BCMS, must also be controlled. Auditors are likely to consider any significant omission a nonconformity, so careful judgement is required.

Satisfying auditors is not the only consideration. There is a fine line between a needlessly burdensome approach to document control and one that is too lax, and both present their own difficulties. Too burdensome, and maintaining the system will consume excessive resources; staff will find it onerous and be disinclined to participate; and you will forever be fighting the impression that the BCMS is merely a vast collection of documents that get in the way of day-to-day operations. Too lax, and the BCMS (and therefore, the continuity plan that arises from it) will be prone to error; it will be harder to achieve business continuity goals and objectives; and staff engagement may drift towards a state of casual disinterest.

Your goal should be to find a balance between the two positions that ensures the BCMS meets requirements and delivers on objectives without being so onerous or laid-back as to pose a risk to the effectiveness of the system. This is a challenge faced by every management system, but one that a BCMS is perhaps more prone to than others – the need to document the continuity plan and the detailed workings it derives from, the exercise programme, etc., naturally results in a larger suite of documentation than might be expected under, for example, ISO 9001.

Creating, updating and controlling documented information

There are five requirements for documented information (and four other aspects that must be addressed as appropriate, which we will cover later). These are as follows:

1. Identification and description.

2. Format.
3. Review and approval.
4. Availability and suitability for use.
5. Adequate protection.

All five of these requirements must be met for all documented information within your BCMS. Omissions will almost certainly result in a nonconformity from any competent auditor.

Identification and description

Identification refers to document names, titles or (unique) reference numbers. Many organisations opt to use both a title and a unique number, the latter of which is often tied to the specific clause within the Standard (e.g. 'BCMS DOC 5.2 Acme Corporation Business Continuity Policy'). This makes it easy to identify the purpose of the document (regardless of whether the reader is familiar with the Standard) and allows the clause the document satisfies to be easily located.

In smaller organisations, titles or names alone may be sufficient, with no need for unique reference numbers. Larger organisations may already operate a document control system of some kind, and simply fold the BCMS documents into an existing reference number system. If you already use a specific naming method for internal documents, it may be better to use and expand on that rather than develop something new that may result in confusion.

Format

Format is simple: whatever your organisation commonly uses that is appropriate for the document concerned. Most organisations use Microsoft Office and Adobe formats

(.docx, .xlsx, .pdf, etc.), and this is perfectly fine. There is little need for concern in respect of this requirement, it will usually be met as a matter of course as the documents are created.

That said, if you take a 'creative' route towards some of your documentation, have a mind to this requirement. Documenting your business continuity policy in a video, for example, would certainly be a unique and creative approach, but it is arguably not the most accessible as it requires a computer or other device to watch it. It would therefore be sensible to maintain a separate, more 'traditional' document in tandem so that you can make the policy easily available to those without access to the hardware necessary to view the video (though this will also necessitate keeping them both up to date, which naturally imposes additional resource implications).

Review and approval

All documented information should be approved before it is put into use, and reviewed periodically to ensure it is still fit for use. Approval involves a check or review by an appropriate person – top management for high-level policies, the business continuity manager or an equivalent role for key BCMS procedures, etc. – to ensure the document still meets requirements. The date of approval and some mechanism indicating that the person responsible has approved it (e.g. name or signature) should be marked on the document, so it is immediately visible that the document has been approved, when the last review took place and when the next review is due.

5: Support

Availability and suitability for use

Availability and suitability for use is another factor of documented information that most organisations will find occurs as a matter of course – after all, having made policies and procedures, you are unlikely to go out of your way to make them unavailable to those who need to use them. Provided that the documentation is accessible at the point of need (including high-level documents such as policies) and not fraught with difficulty if you attempt to use them, you will have little difficulty with this requirement.

There is, however, one sense in which this requirement takes on greater importance within a BCMS than in other management systems. The BCP and any other documented information on which the plan relies must be available to those who need to use it in the event of a disruption. This will likely involve retaining copies at multiple locations to provide redundancy in case the disruption affects the location in which they are stored. Additionally, if you have employees whose native language differs from that used to create your documentation, then you may need to arrange for translations to ensure suitability for use.

Adequate protection

Adequate protection refers to ensuring the confidentiality, integrity and proper use of your documented information. If anyone in the organisation can delete the only copy of your BCP, key procedures or other documents (whether intentionally or otherwise) simply by clicking a mouse, then there is a significant risk to the BCMS and, potentially, to the organisation's ability to recover should a disruption occur. The same is true if those documents can be modified by anyone in the organisation, especially if there is no way to track what changes have been made.

There are a number of ways to ensure that documented information is properly protected. Using (nominally) protected document formats such as .pdf, or more robust technologies such as digital signatures or document control software, can help prevent or reduce the risk of inadvertent or malicious alteration. Measures such as document safes and lockable filing cabinets can reduce the risk of physical damage and improper access. Retaining a master copy in a safe location (whether electronic or physical) and keeping backups guards against the risk of deletion. It should go without saying that all your internal and externally facing networks should be protected by adequate cyber security measures (whether you operate a BCMS or not) as a matter of course.

'Proper use' may seem like a nebulous term, but it is a key part of this requirement. You must ensure that the documents in use are up to date and that you prevent the use of out of date or otherwise incorrect versions. This may require spot checks as part of, or in addition to, the internal audit programme, as using an older, inaccurate version of (for example) the BCP or a key procedure could have significant negative effects. Incorrect, or even malicious use of documents – such as an employee deliberately misinterpreting them or even leaking them to a competitor – must also be guarded against.

Distribution, storage, control and retention

The remaining requirements for document control (clause 7.5.3.2 of the Standard) must be addressed 'as applicable'. These requirements are as follows:

1. Distribution, access, retrieval and use.
2. Storage and preservation (including preservation of legibility).
3. Control of changes.
4. Retention and disposition.

There is also a requirement to identify and control "documented information of external origin" that is necessary for the planning and operation of the BCMS. This is not an 'as applicable' requirement like the list above, but rather a mandatory one. Documents of external origin should be treated in the same manner as your own documents, though you may have to work within some limitations, such as the version number being outside your control. Of course, if your organisations does not make use of any external documentation, then this requirement would not apply, but the chances of this are extremely low.

Distribution, access, retrieval and use

The first requirement should pose little difficulty, and largely boils down to ensuring the documented information is available at the point of need, accessible to those who will need to use it and inaccessible to those who do not (especially for documents containing sensitive information). The systems through which you achieve this are up to you, but intranets and shared document repositories are common methods of ensuring controlled distribution and access.

Storage and preservation

Much of the documentation in organisations today is electronic, and most organisations operate a backup system. If this is the case in your organisation, then storage and preservation may, in principle, be satisfied. However, you should review your backup and storage arrangements (both electronic and physical) to ensure that key BCMS documents and all the information necessary to recover from a disruption are included when backups are performed. You should also determine whether the frequency of backups is adequate, especially in respect of the information you would need to recover from a disruption.

Preservation is generally more relevant to hard copy documents than to electronic ones. Storing hard copy documents in direct sunlight, damp areas or other unsuitable locations can result in damage that could render those documents unreadable or otherwise unusable. It is therefore critical that hard copy storage accounts for the inherently fragile nature of the medium, especially in respect of documents that are stored for long periods.

Electronic documents are less prone to physical preservation concerns, though it is not true to say that they are immune, and electronic preservation has risks also. Storing documents in obscure proprietary formats, for example, could result in major problems if the owner of the format goes out of business and the software to read those documents becomes unavailable. Storing documents in a format that allows untracked modification can also be a problem, as unauthorised changes can render a document ineffective or unusable. Finally, electronic backups should be stored somewhere safe – even the most extensive backups will do you little good if the hardware containing it (whether portable drives, magnetic data tapes, or another medium) is destroyed or rendered unusable through water damage, fire, poor environmental control, etc.

Cloud storage and backups are becoming increasingly common, and although the use of Cloud services may resolve issues surrounding safe storage and retention, they also introduce others. You will need to ensure that the Cloud provider's storage locations are secure and protected against environmental damage, and develop a clear plan for what to do if the Cloud provider goes out of business, is hit by a cyber attack or is affected by disruptions of its own.

Control of changes

Perhaps the most important item on the list, and one likely to be examined by auditors, is control of changes. Uncontrolled changes to BCMS documents can place the organisation's recovery at risk, so almost all documented information – policies, plans, procedures, risk assessments, etc. – should be subject to change control as a safeguard against accidental and unauthorised modification.

Change control invariably involves marking the version number on each page of the document, ideally in the header or footer. The first iteration of a document will be version one, the second version two, etc. Some organisations differentiate between documents that are in a draft state and those that are ready for publication, often by assigning draft documents a version number lower than one (e.g. 0.1, 0.2, etc., indicating different stages of the drafting process), and uprating the version to a whole number at the point of publication (1.0). Later minor revisions are then marked as version 1.1, 1.2, etc., with major revisions moving to the next whole number (2.0, etc.).

This method means that the version is immediately visible on all pages of the document. This is especially important for hard copy documents, since pages can easily be replaced or lost, or shuffled in with different versions of the same document. You will also need a record of some kind that shows the current version of each item of documented information and the date of the most recent change, so that you can compare documents against the record and determine if the version in use is the correct one. Small and medium-sized organisations with a relatively small number of documents often use a spreadsheet for this purpose.

Document sharing libraries such as Microsoft SharePoint offer another, albeit partial, solution to change control. These allow document version numbers to be tracked in the software and provide access to older versions, making it easy to track the lifecycle of documents and largely doing away with the need for a separate index containing the current version and date of change. However, most of them do not automatically mark the document version on or in the document itself, so it is necessary to include the impending version change in the document before it is saved and the version increased within the software.

Controlling records requires a slightly different approach. Records store process outputs and other information (e.g. audit reports, measurement results, meeting minutes) and hence are usually updated far more frequently than policies or procedures. This means that in most cases, it is not practical to apply version control in the same way as you would a policy or procedure, because you would increase the version so rapidly as to become meaningless.

The best approach for records is often to apply version control to the record *template* (i.e. the base document you use to record the information in), but not to the individual data entries. This allows you to see when the template has been updated (e.g. to add a new category of data), and thus provides some measure of control, while avoiding the need to increase the version of the document itself each time new data is added.

Retention and disposition

'Retention and disposition' of documented information refers to how long and in what form it is stored. Most organisations will be familiar with the need to keep documents and records for extended periods, and legal requirements in this respect are common (e.g. retaining certain financial records for a minimum of five years).

It is likely that your organisation already takes steps to retain documentation over the long term. Most organisations operate some form of archiving and storage procedure for hard copy and electronic media, and in such cases, that procedure can simply be adapted to include the documentation generated by the BCMS.

If you do not have such a procedure, you will need to create one. It should define what documentation is retained, for how long, the format it will be retained in and where it will be retained. As part of developing the procedure, you should identify any legal requirements for retaining information and ensure that they are accounted for.

Archives and retained documents, whatever format they are in, should be kept off-site where possible to minimise the risk of loss during a disruption. The off-site location should be secure and protected against environmental damage, cyber attacks and any other potential hazard.

Documents of external origin

Planning and operating the BCMS will inevitably rely on a number of documents created by other parties. If your continuity plan uses externally contracted premises to assist recovery, for example, then there will be contracts and other documents outlining the capacity, functionality and responsibilities in respect of that service. There may also be documentation from suppliers, service providers and other interested parties that is relevant to the BCMS in some capacity – user instructions, specifications, drawings, lists of compatible components or software, service level agreements (SLAs), to name but a few.

This documentation must be identified and controlled alongside your own documented information. It should be accounted for in backup and retention procedures, subject to change control and appropriately preserved. You should also check from time to time that the version you hold is up to date and take steps to acquire the latest version if one is available.

CHAPTER 6: OPERATION

8.1 Operational planning and control

Earlier in this book, we discussed how to identify the context of the organisation and the requirements of interested parties, and determine the actions that arise from them. Clause 8.1 of the Standard requires that you "plan, implement and control" the processes necessary to achieve those actions, and to create and maintain the BCMS. To do this, it expects that you will:

a) Define criteria for these processes;
b) Implement and control the processes in line with the criteria; and
c) Keep documented information to ensure that the processes are carried out.

The criteria referenced are measurement criteria (the metrics by which you will measure the performance and effectiveness of the processes) – and development and implementation criteria (the methods by which you ensure that processes account for the relevant requirements, and are implemented in such a way that they achieve the intended goals). Measurement criteria should ensure that measurements provide useful information and focus on relevant aspects of the process, while development and implementation criteria should ensure that a process designed to meet stakeholder requirements actually does so.

To get the best out of this requirement, define development and implementation criteria before you begin to develop relevant processes, and define measurement criteria during development of a relevant process. This ensures that the process is designed with the relevant requirements in mind, and ensures that any issues with the process that make measurement difficult can be resolved before it is finalised.

Once you have defined the processes and their associated criteria, you need to implement and integrate them so that they become a permanent fixture of your operations. This can take some time during the initial implementation project, depending on the scale of the organisation and its BCMS. Once implemented, you can then evaluate the processes according to the criteria and adjust as necessary. The results of checks against the criteria should be treated as documented information in line with c) above, along with – where possible – the outputs of those procedures.

Change management

Section 8.1 also requires that you control planned changes to the BCMS and review the consequences of unintended changes. Despite the importance of this requirement, it is notably understated.

Although the Standard does not explicitly mandate how you should control changes, most organisations develop a formal change management procedure to account for this requirement. Such a procedure should define how changes are planned and identified, and the stages of investigation, analysis, mitigation (where necessary) and review that will occur.

Change management procedures do not need to be complex to be effective. Although the analysis stage usually bears some resemblance to common risk assessment methods, there is no need to assign scores or develop detailed risk/impact grids (though of course, you can if you want to).

Whatever method you use, the analysis stage should always evaluate the potential impact of a change on three key aspects: the impact on the organisation and its operations, on the BCMS and its processes, and on BCPs.

Change management is not a 'one-off' exercise. Some changes will not reveal their full impact immediately, and even those for which the potential impact seems clear may produce further, unexpected impacts over time. It is critical to review the impact of changes once they are implemented and operating to verify whether things did turn out as predicted, and whether any unexpected impacts occurred. There is no set timescale for this because each change is different, so the procedure should allow for the review period to be set on an individual basis. Regular change planning and review meetings should be scheduled to examine newly proposed changes and review the impact of changes that have been implemented. Mitigation efforts can be routed through the organisation's continual improvement processes or operated separately.

The procedure will also need to account for unanticipated changes – those that arise from changes in the business environment, the changing requirements of interested parties, newly introduced legislation and other factors both within and outside the organisation's control. The consequences of such changes should be analysed and, where necessary, mitigated, just as for planned changes. The outputs of the change procedure (and the procedure itself) should be maintained as documented information.

Some organisations may consider a formal change management procedure onerous. One of the more common objections, aside from the Standard not explicitly mandating one, is that the organisation has operated perfectly well without change control for a number of years and can continue to do so.

There are two routes to overcome such an argument. The first is to examine recent changes and look for evidence of unexpected (usually negative) impacts. If you identify instances where change has resulted in a negative impact, then you have a stronger argument for the necessity of a formal procedure. If you do not, then it is very likely that an informal procedure exists, and you can then make the case for formalising that procedure to improve its effectiveness and help avoid future unexpected impacts.

Although it is possible to meet this requirement via an informal method, demonstrating to an auditor that you are doing so can be challenging. A competent auditor will (justifiably) ask how you can be sure that all relevant impacts are considered, or how you can ensure that you evaluate impacts and review mitigating actions in a systematic, repeatable manner if the relevant criteria are not defined and documented. If you do opt for an informal system, be prepared to answer these, and similar questions.

Control of suppliers and outsourced processes

The final requirement under 8.1 is, like the requirement to control changes, deceptively understated. No organisation is an island, and the business continuity programme must extend its boundaries beyond the organisation to its supply chain to be effective. Yet a casual reader of the Standard could be forgiven for underestimating the importance of the matter, given that ISO 22301 devotes only a single line to the subject.

Ensuring that outsourced processes and the wider supply chain are effectively controlled is perhaps one of the most challenging aspects of implementing a BCMS.

It is likely that a significant proportion of your activities rely directly or indirectly on your suppliers, and from a business continuity perspective, you are as responsible for outsourced activities as you are for in-house ones, if they support your ability to deliver products or services within the scope of the BCMS.

As you undertake the BIA process described later in the Standard, you will almost certainly identify critical dependencies on, and continuity risks associated with, your supply chain that need to be controlled to ensure successful recovery. The requirement to control the supply chain and outsourced processes is a prompt to develop supplier control mechanisms (or review the suitability of any existing ones) so that they are ready when needed.

In an ideal world, all your suppliers would be certified to ISO 22301. In the real world, however, this is the exception rather than the rule. As a result, you will need to work with your suppliers to develop solutions that meet the needs of both parties.

Unfortunately, many suppliers will resist such efforts. Large suppliers often operate on a 'take it or leave it' basis, since they are big enough that they do not have to care about the needs of a small subset of customers. They will point you towards their existing measures (if they have any) and dismiss or ignore any further requests.

Smaller suppliers will often push back too, but for different reasons. The most common objection is that the supplier does not have the resources and/or capital to implement continuity measures, but you may also encounter suppliers who take great offence at the mere suggestion that they should do more simply because you've decided to adopt ISO 22301, regardless of any operational or cost impact.

To effectively face such a challenge, tact and diplomacy are necessary. Many organisations require suppliers to work under SLAs and other contractual arrangements, and where this is the case, extending those arrangements to include continuity provisions is usually easier by virtue of the precedent.

Maintaining good relationships with suppliers is key to ensuring engagement with business continuity requirements. It may be necessary to provide resources, support and guidance, especially if they are approaching business continuity for the first time, and you should make allowances (at least initially) for early mistakes and difficulties. Provided you make it clear that you do not expect them to bear all the burden and that you are willing to work with them and help them implement the suggested measures, many organisations will be happy to at least consider continuity measures.

For particularly intractable suppliers, you may need to make hard decisions. Organisations using the 'take it or leave it' approach that already operate a BCMS will usually be willing to provide some information on their methods, even when they are unwilling (or unable) to modify or adopt new measures on your behalf. You can then evaluate the information provided and determine if it meets your requirements (or whether your requirements can be modified to accommodate the supplier's approach). If the supplier does not have existing business continuity measures and refuses to implement them, then no amount of effort to convince them is likely to make any difference, and it is usually better to consider alternative suppliers than take a gamble on a manifestly uncooperative one.

If you have no other choice but to use an uncooperative supplier, then your BCP will need to account for the risk in some way (e.g. retaining extra stocks to allow you time to find an alternative supplier). However, it is better to avoid being in such a position in the first place – single sources of failure in critical parts of the supply chain are a significant risk and should be eliminated whenever possible.

Evaluating supplier continuity

When evaluating a supplier's continuity measures, do not rely solely on questionnaires or other indirect methods. These are prone to evasion and inflated claims, and often fail to reflect the recipient's true situation. In-person visits and audits (whether formal or informal) are far more effective at determining the facts of the matter and should be used wherever possible. Non-disclosure agreements may help to overcome common concerns about intellectual property or other sensitive information.

Examine the aspects of the supplier's operations that support your business. If it produces components that you use in a physical manufacturing process, then you might verify that it has backup tooling, secondary production lines, backup facilities, etc., to ensure that supply of those components is not vulnerable to disruption. If the supplier operates a Cloud service used by your organisation, then you might query its uptime history and related service provisions, backup procedures and functionality, and other related factors.

Whatever measures you take to control your supply chain, you should ensure that they are described in writing and given effect through contracts or agreements. Contracts and agreements should be reviewed by legal advisors before use in all cases to avoid disputes or other problems.

Certificated suppliers

Given the problems that can arise when working with suppliers to ensure adequate control, it is tempting to assume that you do not need to apply additional controls to suppliers with an ISO 22301 certificate. Although it is certainly true that a supplier certified to ISO 22301 will have a far better understanding of business continuity and will be much more likely to be responsive to your own control requirements, it does not necessarily mean that its BCMS is perfect or that you need take no action. All audits are based on sampling and the certificate alone does not guarantee that everything is as it should be.

You should always check that the certification body that issued the certificate is accredited by a national accreditation body (United Kingdom Accreditation Service (UKAS) in the UK; ANSI National Accreditation Board (ANAB) in the US, etc.). Unaccredited certification carries no guarantee that the certification body is applying the Standard correctly or in a manner that ensures objectivity and independence, and should be viewed with caution. A common red flag that indicates an unaccredited certificate, beyond the conspicuous absence of an appropriate accreditation body logo, is excessive validity periods. Most accredited certificates will only be valid for a maximum of three years – anything longer should trigger a closer examination.

It is important to remember that it is possible to benefit from business continuity measures without seeking certification against ISO 22301. Pushing for all your suppliers to achieve certification is a luxury open only to large organisations with significant buying power and economic heft, and taking such an approach without that level of influence, or with no regard to the circumstances of individual suppliers, will likely cause more problems than it solves.

8.2 BIA and risk assessment

To effectively plan recovery from disruption, you need to determine which activities must be recovered and the necessary parameters for their recovery (how quickly, with what resources, etc.), and the types of disruptions your organisation can reasonably expect to face.

Clause 8.2.1 of the Standard requires the organisation to implement and maintain "systematic processes" to analyse business impact and undertake risk assessment of potential disruptive events. Although it does not explicitly state that those processes must be 'documented information' – it is implied by the various control requirements in Clause 8.1 – these processes are central to the effectiveness of the BCMS and should always be controlled in line with the requirements in part 7.5.

8.2.1 also makes clear that the outputs of both the BIA and the risk assessment process must be reviewed at planned intervals, and after any significant change to the organisation or its operational context. These reviews are critical to the ongoing effectiveness of the BCMS, but are inevitably time consuming, so it is important to schedule them as far in advance as possible and ensure the participants have the time available to conduct them. It is beneficial to conduct the reviews before any upcoming management review (see chapter 9), so that top management can discuss any significant changes or new items at the management review meeting.

8.2.2 BIA

BIA is the process of identifying the activities your organisation performs to deliver products or services and understanding how each one could be affected by disruptive events. It allows you to identify the activities that must be prioritised to ensure an effective recovery and is one of the most critical procedures in the BCMS.

There is no avoiding the fact that BIA is a time-consuming and sometimes complex process, especially when performed for the first time while implementing a BCMS. It is important to ensure that enough time and resources are available to conduct the BIA in a thorough and systematic manner, as the outputs of the process feed directly into development of the continuity plan and strongly influence its overall effectiveness.

Fortunately, the requirements in 8.2.2 also double as a template around which you can design your BIA process. If you account for all the requirements in the order they are presented and heed the guidance in the following sections of this book, you should end up with a robust BIA process that will satisfy auditors.

Impact types and criteria

The first step in the BIA process is to determine criteria for evaluating disruptive impacts, and the types of impacts that are relevant to the organisation. Although the specific types and criteria for impacts will naturally differ depending on the nature of the organisation, the approach is generally the same.

When an activity is interrupted, there is a corresponding negative impact. In most cases, the longer the interruption, the larger the impact – and at some point, even if initially tolerable, that impact will become intolerable. It is therefore necessary to analyse the organisation's activities to discover how and when an interruption results in intolerable impact so that critical activities can be prioritised during recovery.

To ensure a consistent understanding of impact, and a consistent approach towards prioritisation, we need to define criteria against which to compare impacts of different types. To do this, begin by defining the types of impact that could feasibly occur. For many, the first thought will be of financial impact, but there are many other types to consider: reputational, contractual, operational, legal/regulatory, environmental, service level reduction – to name but a few. The outputs of the work done on the context of the organisation and the requirements of interested parties can be of use in determining impact types that may not be immediately obvious.

Once you have a list of the possible impact types your organisation may be subject to, the next step is to establish an impact scale for each one in relatively broad terms so that the users of the process can accurately judge the severity of a given impact. A five-point scale is commonly used, and while you are free to choose as many levels as you wish, it pays not to have too many or too few. Scales with three or fewer levels rarely provide enough granularity to support effective decision-making, and scales with more than five tend to over-complicate matters.

Once you have determined appropriate scales for each potential impact type, consolidate them into a single matrix for ease of use, and incorporate the matrix into the procedure.

Table 1: Example Impact Matrix

Level	Description	Financial (£)	Reputational	Environmental
1	Insignificant	< 25,000	< 50% increase in customer complaints	Temporary damage; no risk to health or wildlife
2	Minor	25,001 to 75,000	> 50% increase in customer complaints; brief local media coverage	Temporary damage; minor localised risk to health or wildlife
3	Moderate	75,001 to 200,000	> 100% increase in complaints; sustained local media coverage	Medium-term damage; medium localised risk to health or wildlife
4	Major	200,001 to 500,000	National media coverage; complaints to authorities, short-term damage to brand	Long-term damage; major localised risk to health or wildlife

5	Catastrophic	> 500,000	National media coverage, product withdrawal, long-term damage to brand	Extensive long-term or permanent damage; widespread major risk to health or wildlife

Identifying activities

Now that you have a comprehensive impact matrix, the next step is to identify the activities your organisation performs that support delivery of products and services in scope of the BCMS. This can be a time-consuming exercise and one that is prone to oversimplification, so it is important to approach this in a systematic, thorough manner.

Because the process is time-intensive, there is a balance to be found between identifying every single activity and only those that are relevant. There is often a temptation to arbitrarily identify key activities and their supporting resources without performing a detailed analysis, but this must be resisted – experienced auditors will identify this approach quickly, and using it imperils the effectiveness of your recovery.

There are several methods you can use to effectively identify activities, and it is best to deploy a combination of all of them to ensure you do not miss anything relevant. Your starting point should be the scope of the BCMS, as this defines the activities within scope of the exercise at the highest level (e.g. all services provided by the organisation, or all physical products produced at site A).

The next step is to consider the organisation from the top down as a collection of dependent entities. Look at each department or operational function in turn and list their main activities to develop a broad, high-level picture that you can build on in the next stage: production site A produces these five products; service centre B provides support to these geographical regions, etc.

You should then talk to the people in those departments to understand the detail of their activities. Questionnaires, brainstorming sessions and one-to-one meetings can all help identify aspects of activities that the earlier stages of this process cannot. Collaborate with managers and employees to develop an activity map so you have a clear visual representation of the connectivity between activities. It can be helpful to use software to develop the final map, as maps for all but the smallest organisations will likely be very large and unwieldy on paper – though the pen and paper approach works fine when mapping individual activities.

Assess impact over time

The next step in the BIA process is to determine the impact over time that a disruption will cause to each of the activities identified in the previous step. The impact of a disruption on any given activity is rarely linear, and with enough time, there will come a point at which the organisation considers the impact unacceptable. By evaluating the impact over time on each activity and seeing how quickly each one becomes unacceptable, you can determine which activities need to be prioritised during recovery.

To determine impact over time, plot one or more of the impact criteria against a timeline for each activity and estimate the impact at each stage of the timeline to create the activity's unique impact profile. The timeline you choose should account for the nature of the products or services your organisation offers, and allow enough granularity to classify the impacts at key stages. The timeline for a manufacturer of physical products might range from one full day to several weeks, but the timeline for an operator of a large-scale Cloud service (for which there is often an expectation of greater than 99% uptime) might range from minutes to hours.

In some cases, it may be appropriate to treat a group of related activities (e.g. all production lines) as one activity for the purposes of this analysis. This can save time and is perfectly acceptable provided that the impact is the same or very similar for all activities in the group – if it is not, or if some related activities are manifestly more critical than others, then you should analyse them individually.

You will need a range of inputs to properly determine the impact on an activity, but your first port of call should be top and operational management, as they are best placed to understand what the effect on the organisation could be. Talking to relevant employees is also worthwhile, as they are often aware of smaller but no less critical aspects that may escape those not who do not perform the activity regularly.

When determining impact, you will need to account for both internal and external factors that can affect the outcome. For example, if the disruption of an activity has relatively low financial impact initially, but could result in loss of a major contract if it lasted for a month or more, then the impact profile might look something like this:

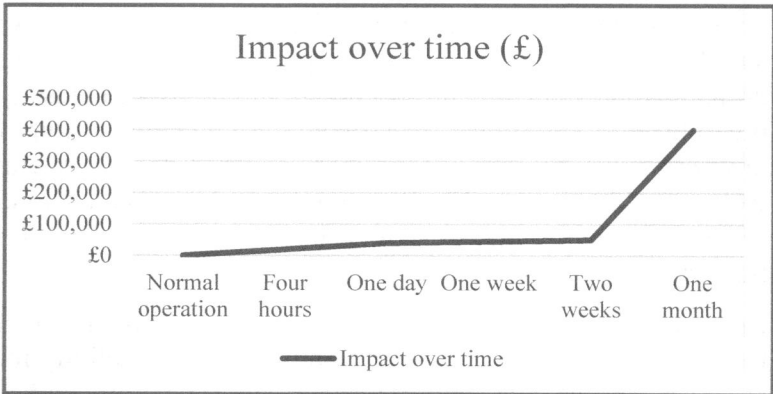

Figure 1: Example financial impact over time

Where an activity is subject to multiple impact types, it is up to you to decide how best to represent them in a single value that you can map against the criteria. You could use the value from the impact type with the highest result, take the average of all the results at each point in the time frame or estimate the total impact of all the different types – or any other method you deem appropriate (provided you can explain the logic behind it to an auditor).

Once you have done this for all your activities, enter the data into a table so that you can easily compare the results.

Table 2: Impact Table Comparison

Division	Activity	Impact over time				
		Four hours	One day	One week	Two weeks	One month
Production	Production line 1	1	2	2	2	4
Production	Production line 2	1	2	3	3	3
Production	Production line 3	1	2	3	3	4
Finance	Accounts payable	1	2	3	4	5
Finance	Payroll	1	1	1	3	5
Sales	Call centre	1	3	4	5	5
Sales	Order processing	1	2	3	4	4
Service	Service desk	1	1	1	2	3

Determine maximum tolerable period of disruption (MTPD)

With the impact profiles for your activities recorded, you can determine the MTPD.[8] This is the point at which the impact of a disruption becomes unacceptable (for whatever reason). You can do this for each activity after you have plotted the impact profile or wait until you have profiles for all relevant activities, though the latter is often easier as you can get all the relevant people in one place and work through several activities in the same session.

Some organisations define the MTPD by drawing an arbitrary line at a certain level of the impact criteria beyond which the impact is unacceptable – for example, anything more than two, or anything more than three. Alternatively, some evaluate the various contributing factors and define a unique MTPD for each activity.

---

[8] ISO 22301: 2019 no longer includes definitions of BC-specific terms such as MTPD, recovery time objective (RTO), etc., and notes in the text that the generic descriptions, e.g. "the time frame within which the impacts of not resuming activities would become unacceptable" can be referred to using these terms, but that it is not mandatory.

BC terminology has evolved over the years and while the concepts behind the terms used have largely remained the same, the specific terminology often differs across industries. One organisation may refer to the maximum tolerable period of disruption as MTPD, while another refers to it as 'maximum acceptable outage' (MAO). Both terms mean the same thing, but the presence of multiple equivalent terms has resulted in much confusion over the years, and the shift away from such specific terminology in the Standard is intended to reduce that confusion. This book uses the terms in the Standard for ease of reading and interpretation only – there is no harm in using MAO instead of MTPD if that is the preference within your organisation.

Setting an arbitrary limit for MTPD saves time in the BIA but is also less precise. Defining individual MTPDs is more time consuming but allows greater precision in the next stage of the BIA. Arbitrary limits can be appropriate for large groups of similar or related activities but should be avoided entirely during the first BIA (performed during BCMS implementation), as that BIA is intended to be more exploratory than those that follow it.

Whichever method you use, ensure that you account for any activity-specific legal and contractual requirements (e.g. laws that mandate specific uptime requirements, or service level requirements in SLAs) when determining the MTPD for an activity. It may be that the operational impact of a disruption on a given activity is tolerable for longer than law or contract permit; where this is the case, the MTPD should be set at the duration required by the law or contract concerned.

Table 3 shows the MTPD for a group of activities where the MTPD has been set using the arbitrary method at anything higher than level two of the impact criteria.

Table 3: MTPD = Greater than 2

Activity	MTPD	Impact over time				
		Four hours	One day	One week	Two weeks	One month
Production line 1	One month	1	2	2	2	4
Production line 2	One week	1	2	3	3	3
Production line 3	One week	1	2	3	3	4
Accounts payable	One week	1	2	3	4	5
Payroll	Two weeks	1	1	1	3	5
Call centre	One day	1	3	4	5	5
Order processing	One week	1	2	3	4	4
Service desk	One month	1	1	1	2	3

Determine recovery time objectives (RTOs) and minimum capacity

Now that you know how long it takes before the impact of a disruption on a given activity becomes unacceptable (the MTPD), the next step in the BIA process is to determine how quickly you must recover each activity if a disruption occurs. This is known as the RTO.

There are several factors to consider, and some documentation to assemble, when determining RTOs. The first factor is whether, to avoid exceeding the MTPD, it is possible to recover the activity in full or only partially. In most cases, the goal is partial recovery, since full recovery of an activity may take an extremely long time (or be entirely unfeasible) and the organisation needs to get up and running as quickly as possible.

To help understand whether full or partial recovery is necessary (and to comply with the requirement in 8.2.2e to resume activities at a "specified minimum capacity"), you must document the minimum operating capacity for each activity. This necessarily involves understanding the normal operating capacity of those activities – you cannot properly determine one without the other. Documenting the minimum capacity ensures you have a formal basis against which to design the continuity plan, and allows you to see, through testing and exercises, whether the continuity plan delivers that capacity when it is put into action.

The complexity of the activity and the dependencies on which it relies are also relevant factors. A manufacturing activity that relies on specific tooling that is lost during a disruption, for example, cannot be resumed until the tooling is replaced. If the replacement takes four weeks to manufacture and deliver, then the RTO cannot sensibly be shorter than four weeks (unless you have a spare set of tooling). If only one supplier can provide that replacement tooling, then its continuity measures and susceptibility to disruption need to be accounted for as well – not to mention the time needed to install it, set up associated equipment, etc. once it is delivered to your site.

Above all, the RTO should be shorter than the MTPD (otherwise the continuity plan, no matter how well designed, will provide no benefit). If we take the earlier list of example activities and MTPDs, and assign an arbitrary (for the purposes of this example) RTO of half of the MTPD, the result looks like this:

Table 4: Assigning RTOs

Activity	MTPD	RTO
Production line 1	One month	Two weeks
Production line 2	One week	Three days
Production line 3	One week	Three days
Accounts payable	One week	Three days
Payroll	Two weeks	One week
Call centre	One day	Four hours
Order processing	One week	Three days
Service desk	One month	Two weeks

6: Operation

A short note on recovery point objectives (RPOs)

RPOs are described in ISO 22313 as a useful corollary to RTOs, assigned to activities that rely on data or information systems. An RPO defines the amount of data you can afford to lose before you can no longer resume the activity (or put another way, the maximum acceptable period between backups). For example, if it would be impossible to resume an activity after more than 24 hours of data loss, then the RPO is 24 hours, and both the MTPD and the frequency at which backups of that data are created must be less than 24 hours.

RPOs are not mandatory, but they are a useful tool to ensure that information is backed up frequently enough to allow an activity to be recovered. The same analysis used to define the RTO should also highlight the RPO where one is applicable, since you will need to understand the data necessary to perform the activity to be able to document the minimum operational capacity.

Identify prioritised activities

Once you have identified RTOs, you can begin to prioritise the actions you will take during recovery. To begin with, exclude all activities that the organisation does not need to recover during a disruption. You can then reorganise the remaining data to show RTOs in order of increasing length to develop a set of base priorities that you can later modify. Applying this method to the earlier list of activities produces a list like this:

Table 5: RTOs in Order of Increasing Length

Activity	MTPD	RTO
Call centre	One day	Four hours
Order processing	One week	Three days
Production line 2	One week	Three days
Production line 3	One week	Three days
Accounts payable	One week	Three days
Payroll	Two weeks	One week
Production line 1	One month	Two weeks
Service desk	One month	Two weeks

RTOs are not the only consideration, however. In the example above, several activities have the same RTO, but this does not mean they are all equally important – one of those activities may be more crucial to maintaining the organisation's bottom line than the others, and should therefore be prioritised. It may also be the case that an activity with a longer RTO needs to be prioritised over one with a shorter RTO, to meet stakeholder or legal requirements.

These priorities will play a major role in development of your BCP, so it is important to get them right. Where factors other than RTO are relevant, you should record additional information so that the rationale for prioritisation is clear in future BIAs.

Identify resources

Now that you know which activities to prioritise during recovery, you can determine the resources each activity uses on a day-to-day basis. Resources can include people (and any necessary training), facilities (and utilities such as power, water, etc.), tools and equipment, IT systems and software, communication systems, products or components provided by suppliers and partners, and logistics (e.g. delivery capacity, loading areas).

Take care to identify resources that are shared across multiple activities, and those that have a built-in time lag, such as hand-made bespoke components or items that can only be transported by cargo ship. If your activities rely on third-party products or components, you will need to consider how much stock of those items you will need to support the activity through the period of disruption. This is especially important in scenarios where suppliers are themselves disrupted, e.g. during a pandemic.

Data resources play a key role in almost all modern organisations but present a different challenge to that posed by physical resources. Backups may need conversion into a usable format before an activity can be resumed, for example, which may require special equipment or software. Legislation around use and control of personal data must still be complied with during a disruption, so you may need to account for specific IT and physical security controls and the resources necessary to implement them to avoid breaching legal requirements.

6: Operation

Identify dependencies

The final factor in the BIA is to identify the dependencies on which the prioritised activities rely. This can be a particularly complex exercise, especially in larger organisations with lots of concurrent activities, so it is important to keep clear, easy to understand records to avoid confusion and misidentification, and to aid later BIAs.

Some dependencies will be obvious. Customers cannot make payments without a functional payment processing system, for example, and almost all manufacturing relies on components produced by other organisations. Even the most cursory consideration of an activity should highlight these, whether they relate to other activities within the organisation or to activities performed by suppliers and partners.

Hidden dependencies present a greater challenge, as they often remain invisible until a disruption occurs. Identifying these usually involves detailed discussion with those responsible for the activity, as they are best placed to identify the minor but critical factors that may go unnoticed by others.

Top management approval and consolidation

ISO 22301 does not explicitly require you to gain top management approval of the results of the BIA, but doing so is recommended. The results of the BIA directly influence the business continuity strategy and the plan that arises from that strategy, so ensuring top management agreement at this stage helps avoid problems in the future. Management may also wish to alter the order of prioritised activities in line with strategic concerns (though you should ensure that any changes make sense and remain in line with the output of the BIA).

BIA is a complex process that produces a lot of data, which in turn means that it is necessary to present all that data in a clear, accessible manner to avoid mistakes and misinterpretation. It is also a cyclic activity – you must review the BIA periodically to ensure it remains effective for as long as the BCMS is in operation. To that end, it is sensible to consolidate the various outputs into a coherent, stable, and accessible format once the BIA is complete, both to benefit the selection of strategies and solutions for the first BIA and to inform future BIAs.

8.3 Risk assessment

For your organisation to recover effectively from a disruption, you need to understand what kind of disruptive events you might face. The Standard expects you to evaluate and assess the risks disruptive events pose to your prioritised activities and the resources they rely on – only then can you develop appropriate business continuity strategies, solutions and plans to mitigate them. You must have a defined risk assessment process (as per 8.2.3), and it should be maintained as documented information, as it is a critical part of the BCMS.

It is not for this book to describe risk assessment methodology in detail. Most organisations take a qualitative approach, usually involving a three- to five-point likelihood/impact scale of the kind familiar to most managers and management system practitioners. Such an approach is perfectly adequate for the purposes of meeting the requirement, though you may wish to consider performing additional quantitative assessment for those risks that have very large or significant impact potential. It can also be helpful to align your risk assessment criteria to your impact criteria, where possible. If you are unsure about the mechanics and methodology of risk assessment, ISO 31000 provides a useful introduction, and there is a wealth of information available online.[9]

Identifying business continuity risks can be more challenging than risk assessment in other management systems. Alongside more commonplace risks such as fire, flood or cyber attack, the organisation must also consider risks that are far less likely but can still result in a major disruption. This raises the question, especially for new business continuity practitioners, as to where to draw the line between risks that are genuinely out of scope, and those that are extremely unlikely but still relevant to the BCMS.

The unfortunate exemplar of this problem is the COVID-19 pandemic. Although 'pandemic flu' has always been at least nominally 'on the radar' for business continuity practitioners, very few BCMS operators took steps to account for one occurring, on the presumption that a pandemic was so unlikely as to not be worth expending resources on. Some of those practitioners would no doubt argue that COVID-19 is a 'one-off' or 'black swan' event that could not be planned for, but such an argument misses the point – the BCMS is intended to protect against exactly those kinds of events.

Essentially, identification of business continuity risks boils down to a combination of common sense and a detailed understanding of the organisation and how it operates. To use an extreme example, the risk of volcanic eruption is so low as to be irrelevant to an organisation operating out of London

---

[9] ISO 31000:2018 *Risk Management – Guidelines*. Note that this standard is available in read-only format for free at the ISO website: *www.iso.org/standard/65694.html*.

(unless that organisation's products or services rely on a supplier located near to a volcano with a history of recent activity) because it is a geological impossibility. A pandemic on the other hand, although highly unlikely, is subject to no such restriction. It can strike anywhere at any time, so it is still relevant to the BCMS.

Relevant risks will arise in large part from the context of the organisation (and, to a lesser extent, the requirements of interested parties), and the nature of its operations. The risks for a Cloud service provider operating out of an area prone to tornados will be very different to those faced by a chemical manufacturer whose primary site is located on a flood plain. By considering what the organisation does, where and how it does it, and its wider place in the community, alongside relevant local and global events, you should be able to exclude the ludicrous while still ensuring that you capture the risks that matter.

Record the risks you identify in a risk register (which should be maintained as documented information) for ease of evaluation, and so you have something to demonstrate to an auditor. You can then evaluate the likelihood and potential impact of each risk in line with the scale documented in your risk assessment process.

Treating business continuity risks

Experienced practitioners will note the absence of a requirement in 8.2.3 to treat the risks you identify. This is not an omission – the business continuity strategies, solutions and plans you develop in 8.3 of the Standard serve that purpose. However, the risk assessment process will likely identify comparatively minor risks, or components of risks, that can easily be proactively treated, and thereby reduce the number of scenarios for which a formal continuity response is necessary. This aspect should not be neglected – deploying a formal continuity response is no small undertaking, and prevention is always better than cure.

CHAPTER 7: BUSINESS CONTINUITY STRATEGIES AND SOLUTIONS

With the dataset you have generated in the previous chapters, and the information provided by your risk assessment process, you are now in a position to determine the strategies and solutions you will use to respond to disruptive events. Strategies are the structural frameworks that ensure prioritised activities are recovered in line with the defined time frames; solutions are the actions taken to ensure the strategy is realised. Each strategy will comprise one or more solutions, in much the same way that a process comprises one or more actions, and the solutions comprising each strategy will be formalised into plans that the organisation will use should a disruption occur.

The 2012 edition of ISO 22301 referred only to 'business continuity strategy'. Practitioners frequently interpreted this to mean that the Standard expected the development of one large, all-encompassing strategy and accompanying continuity plan, and this notion has been reinforced across much of the media and available guidance ever since.

Although 'grand plans' sound great on paper, in practice they tend to be inflexible and prone to failure. Disruptive events rarely proceed exactly as anticipated, and overly rigid plans tend to collapse when presented with circumstances that do not precisely match the assumptions they were based on. Additionally, because 'grand plans' try to account for every disruptive event the organisation might face, they tend to lack the detail needed to respond to events in a manner that is truly effective.

In the 2019 edition of ISO 22301, the language changed to "strategies and solutions".[10] This helps highlight that business continuity strategies are comprised of specific solutions to specific business continuity risks, and the use of the plural emphasises that having multiple strategies, rather than a single all-encompassing one, is an acceptable way to meet the requirement.

8.3.2 Identification of strategies and solutions

The Standard states that strategies must consider solutions that are applied before, during and after a disruptive incident. Recovering from a loss of power at a data centre, for example, might involve regular backups, uninterruptible power supplies, and alternative server and storage hardware in a different region – three solutions that each deal with a different aspect of the disruption and are employed at different times. The intent is that you consider proactive solutions to business continuity risks, not solely reactive ones, and recognise that recovery often takes place in stages, each of which may require different solutions.

ISO 22301 contains a list of requirements that are intended to guide the identification of strategies and solutions, as follows:

a) Meet the requirements to continue and recover prioritized activities within the identified time frames and agreed capacity;
b) Protect the organization's prioritized activities;
c) Reduce the likelihood of disruption;
d) Shorten the period of disruption;

---

[10] ISO 22301:2019, 8.3.

e) *Limit the impact of disruption on the organization's products and services;*
f) *Provide for the availability of adequate resources.*[11]

You should consider all possible solutions in light of these requirements and ensure that any selected meet at least one of them. If a given solution does not meet one or more of these requirements, it is likely to be unsuitable.

8.3.3 Selection of strategies and solutions

When selecting solutions, the Standard again includes requirements to guide the process. Solutions shall:

a) *Meet the requirements to continue and recover prioritized activities within the identified time frames and agreed capacity;*
b) *Consider the amount and type of risk the organization may or may not take;*
c) *Consider associated costs and benefits.*[12]

For each activity, determine solutions based on the nature of the activity, the MTPD, the RTO and the organisation's business continuity objectives. Remember that your solutions should include those applied before, during and after a disruptive incident – some activities may require multiple solutions operating consecutively or simultaneously to account for their entire recovery timeline. It may also be the case that a single solution is applicable to multiple activities.

---

[11] ISO 22301:2019, 8.3.2.

[12] ISO 22301:2019, 8.3.3.

Map the solutions against your activities to ensure that each activity has a solution or solutions that cover the whole recovery timeline. It can be helpful to highlight solutions that are applicable to more than one activity in a different colour to aid strategic planning. Save room in your spreadsheet (or whatever you are using to map solutions to activities) for the resources each solution requires, but do not identify those resources yet – that will follow in the next section.

Managers with a keen financial eye will be pleased to see "associated costs and benefits" included within the selection criteria. In line with risk management practice, the Standard expects that the cost of solutions is proportionate to the risk.

From solutions to strategies

Now that you have solutions for each prioritised activity, it is time to consider strategies. These are essentially high-level summaries of the actions you will take in a given scenario – the detail of the strategy, such as the order of actions and processes etc., will be defined in the associated continuity plan.

To develop strategies, begin with the business continuity risks you identified during the risk assessment and assign each one to a broad category based on their outcome. For example, place all risks that prevent access to the premises (fire, flood, structural failure, etc.) into one group, and all risks that would prevent access to your data (cyber attack, ransomware, etc.) into another.

Because the outcome of the events in a category is similar, the strategy to resolve them will also be similar. The order in which you recover activities will be similar and resource use will also be comparable (though there will be some variation based on the specific circumstances), so you can develop a strategy for each category – premises recovery strategy, data recovery strategy, etc. – that accounts for that particular subset of business continuity risks.

This method allows you to cover a large number of risks with a small number of strategies, avoiding not only the problems associated with one large overarching strategy, but also the resource expenditure (and inevitable duplication of effort) that would be required to develop a strategy for each individual risk. Although it may still be necessary to develop standalone strategies for risks that do not fit into one of your categories, the number required should be low.

Although the Standard does not mandate that strategies are maintained as documented information, they are a key part of the BCMS and therefore fall within the "necessary for the effectiveness of the BCMS" component of 7.5.1. Treating them as documented information will also help ensure that the latest available versions are used and provide a history of changes as they evolve over time.

8.3.4 Resource requirements

With solutions mapped to activities and strategies in place for how you will recover those activities, you can then determine the resources each solution will require.

The 2019 edition of ISO 22301 is explicit that resources should be determined for solutions, not strategies. This marks a significant change from the 2012 edition, which focused on determining resources at the strategic level, and is intended to drive a more detailed analysis of the resources needed to ensure recovery.

It is important to remember that the resources an activity uses on a day-to-day basis may not be the same as those needed to ensure recovery. By defining resources for solutions rather than for activities, you ensure that BCMS expenditure is focused on the things you need to recover from a disruption.

People

When planning personnel requirements for a recovery, you need to ensure that enough trained, competent staff are available. Depending on the nature of potential disruptions, you may need to consider training staff on more than one role so that they can step in to fill gaps, or make provision for retraining. If availability of staff is reduced, you may need to consider hiring temporary staff from a third party or making alterations to working conditions so that existing staff can perform their roles from home or from other sites.

Health, safety and well-being should be paramount concerns during any disruption and may require resources such as personal protective equipment or spill control kits. You may also need to consider ancillary resources – if a disruption could result in loss of site access, then transport and logistics to ensure employees can access the backup site, along with necessary amenities at the backup site, (power, water, food and rest facilities, etc.) may be required, for example.

Information and data

All organisations rely on data, whether in electronic or hard copy format, and it is a safe bet that you will need to access your data during a disruption. You will need to ensure that your data is available, which may involve recovering it from backups – where this is the case, make sure you can recover it in enough time to meet any relevant RTOs. If accessing the data requires special software or hardware, this will also need to be available, and you will also need to consider how you will merge any new data with the old once a disruption ends and you return to business as usual.

If your data is in hard copy rather than electronic format, you will need to consider how best to protect it against damage caused by potential disruptions, and how to access it should the need arise. This might involve transferring the data to a digital format so it can be backed up, relocating hard copy files to another site or storage facility, or other suitable methods. You may also need to consider how to store any files generated during the disruption itself, if access to existing storage is prevented.

Throughout the disruption you must ensure that you continue to comply with any legal requirements around the use and storage of data (especially personal data), and ensure the confidentiality, integrity and availability of the data to the same degree as your normal operating environment, as far as is possible.

Physical infrastructure

Planning for physical infrastructure is heavily dependent on the nature of the business continuity risks you face and the size of your organisation. If those risks include events that could damage or otherwise prevent access to your premises, then you will need to consider alternative sites or premises – whether procured in advance (often not feasible because of the expense involved) or procured 'as needed'. Alternatives can include using a secondary site owned by your organisation (e.g. by moving other activities to make room), or one provided by a third party on a defined or ad-hoc basis. You could also consider remote working or outsourcing, where appropriate.

Any secondary site should not be vulnerable to the same risks as the primary site. If the primary site has a major fire risk, then choosing an adjacent building as your alternative site is unlikely to be suitable. For natural disasters such as flooding, it may be necessary to reference geographic information such as water tables and height maps to make sure any secondary site is not also prone to flooding. You will also need to consider your employees' willingness to travel – if your secondary site is 100 miles away, staff are unlikely to want to commute, even for a short period of time.

Any alternative site will require power, water, Internet and communications infrastructure, heating, lighting and other utilities. You will also need to consider furniture: desks, chairs, tables, stools or whatever else is appropriate. These can take time to set up if the site is not already in use or provisioned by a third party, and any setup or installation time should be accounted for in your planning. If you are sharing the site with other companies, there may also be security and confidentiality considerations around data or intellectual property that must be resolved.

Equipment and consumables

Most, if not all, activities require equipment and/or consumables. Hand tools, fixed equipment (e.g. drills, lathes), industrial plant and tooling, stationery and office supplies, safety and personal protective equipment should all be considered in your planning. Components and consumables used in manufacturing processes (epoxies, sealants, etc.) should also be identified at this stage.

Equipment or consumables that are subject to long lead times require careful planning to ensure adequate stock levels for the duration of the disruption. It may be necessary to provide for additional storage space (perhaps at a different site to reduce risk) to ensure that day-to-day operations are not themselves disrupted. Where activities rely on hand-made or bespoke components, it may be necessary to consider alternative suppliers or other options, such as SLAs (or convincing them to implement their own business continuity measures).

ICT systems

The modern office relies on IT systems, so it is almost certain that you will need to provide for adequate IT and communication facilities during a disruption. Desktop and laptop PCs, peripherals and printers, networking and storage, software and applications all need to be considered, along with necessary network and IT security measures to ensure data protection and compliance with relevant legislation during recovery. Alternative communication and connectivity provision should also be considered, as some disruptions may result in the loss of existing communications infrastructure.

Where there are business continuity risks associated with networking or data storage, take care to ensure that those risks cannot be inadvertently (or intentionally) transferred to systems involved in the recovery process after a disruption has occurred. Network segregation, least-privilege principles and other information security methods can be used to achieve this.

Finally, legacy software and systems that are not compatible with modern IT equipment or operating systems pose a particular challenge in a recovery scenario. It can be difficult – especially at short notice – to acquire the necessary hardware or software, so you may need to retain at least one set of backup legacy equipment (or develop an alternative system) so that the activity can continue during a disruption.

Legacy hardware and software often contain publicly available security vulnerabilities. If you have no choice but to maintain legacy software or systems, these should be mitigated as much as is possible before restarting the activity. With the number of cyber attacks increasing each year, such vulnerabilities may constitute continuity risks in and of themselves.

Transportation and logistics

Logistics is one aspect of business continuity planning that is often neglected in favour of more immediate needs, yet it is a key component of all the resources discussed so far. For example, every transfer of equipment or delivery of components to a backup site will involve logistics, whether under your control or that of a third party, and there are considerations around staff transport and access as well.

Logistics under your own control may need special arrangements during a disruption. This includes physical delivery services, service and repair at customer sites, and even face-to-face sales, depending on the organisation and the nature of the disruption. Those outside of your control should be evaluated from a business continuity perspective to see if their arrangements are adequate for the solutions you have identified – if they are not, then it may be necessary to consider alternative providers.

Finance

Finance underpins all organisational projects, and continuity planning is no exception. Solutions must be implemented (as far as is possible) before a disruption occurs and maintained both during a disruption and over the long term, which naturally imposes costs on the organisation. Planning for these costs should take place just as it would for any major project, with defined budgets and oversight by top management.

It is sensible to consider how the organisation will finance itself during a disruption, when incoming funds may be partially reduced or stopped entirely. This is particularly important if your organisation is at risk of prolonged disruption, where income could be impacted for weeks or months, or if disruptions could result in the loss of expensive equipment or stock that must be replaced to allow recovery of prioritised activities. Insurance may play a role in this respect, but business continuity insurance is rarely truly comprehensive, as we discussed in the introduction to this book, and should not be relied on in isolation.

The amount of 'buffer' finance required will depend on the nature of the prioritised activities and the potential disruptions the organisation might face. You may need to provide for transport costs, equipment or goods, expenses related to secondary sites (rental of premises, installation of utilities, etc.), payroll and other factors, not to mention unexpected costs that arise from the specific circumstances of the disruption.

Partners and suppliers

Where prioritised activities rely on goods or services provided by suppliers or partners, you will need to ensure that those goods or services are available throughout a disruption. It will be necessary to evaluate your suppliers' business continuity measures to determine whether additional action is needed to safeguard the operation of your prioritised activities (as noted in chapter 6 of this book).

Consider developing criteria for evaluation of supplier business continuity to allow all suppliers to be judged on the same basis, and to ensure useful metrics can be generated. Work with suppliers to cascade requirements through the entire supply chain as far as is possible, and conduct periodic audits to ensure that they are meeting expectations. It may also be beneficial to include suppliers in business continuity exercises, where appropriate – this is particularly useful for outsourced activities (for which you remain responsible in terms of continuity and the BCMS).

8.3.5 Implementing solutions

Now that you have identified your solutions and the resources they need to function, the next step is to implement as many of those solutions (and associated resources) as possible. Although there will naturally be some aspects that can only be implemented once a disruption has occurred, the more you can do in advance, the better. In cases where it is not practical or cost effective to provide for resources before a disruption occurs, the relationships necessary to ensure procurement should be developed so that if, or when, procurement becomes necessary, it is a smooth and well-planned operation.

Note that 8.3.5 asks you to "implement and maintain" solutions. Depending on the nature of the solutions you have selected, you may need to develop an ongoing maintenance programme to ensure that they continue to operate as expected over time (this is particularly important for solutions that rely on complex equipment or large installations). Any maintenance programme for your solutions should be included in your internal audit programme to ensure that it operates as expected over time.

CHAPTER 8: BCPs AND PROCEDURES

With a significant proportion of your preparations complete, you can now turn your attention to the mechanisms you will use to respond to disruptive incidents. This section of the Standard requires that you create response structures, plans and procedures to guide and control the actions you take during a disruption.

When developing BCMS procedures for use in responding to a disruption, it is important to ensure they meet the requirements laid out in clause 8.4.1 of the Standard. These procedures must:

a) *be specific regarding the immediate steps that are to be taken during a disruption;*
b) *be flexible to respond to the changing internal and external conditions of a disruption;*
c) *focus on the impact of incidents that potentially lead to disruption;*
d) *be effective in minimizing the impact through the implementation of appropriate solutions;*
e) *assign roles and responsibilities for tasks within them.*[13]

Although all good procedures should contain specific steps and define roles and responsibilities for the tasks in question, flexibility is perhaps a less common concern. No disruptive event proceeds exactly as anticipated, however, so it is important that recovery procedures have some degree of flexibility 'built-in' so that they can still be used if the

---

[13] ISO 22301:2019, 8.4.1.

scenario occurring is not quite the same as that originally envisioned.

Arguably the most important thing about recovery procedures – and one that is not listed in the Standard – is that they must be clear and easy to understand. These processes will be used while the organisation is disrupted, in an atmosphere that is likely to be fast-moving, chaotic and constantly changing. Complex and convoluted procedures are prone to misunderstanding and error at the best of times, let alone in such an environment, so the simpler and easier you can make them, the better for your recovery.

When developing recovery procedures, make critical information highly visible (bold text, colours, text boxes, etc.) and keep individual instructions short and to the point. Highlight dependencies (other procedures, documents, records, etc.) and outputs so that the relationship between stages and other processes is clear.

8.4.2 Response structure

Responding effectively to a disruption requires careful decision making and a strategic overview of the organisation. To comply with 8.4.2, you will need to develop a response structure and define one or more teams that are responsible for responding to disruptive events.

The number and size of response teams will depend on the size and scale of your organisation. Smaller organisations may find a single team sufficient; larger organisations or those that operate multiple sites will likely require a larger team, or multiple teams. Where more than one team exists, the relationship between teams and any shared responsibilities should be made explicit (as per clause 8.4.2.2), to avoid the risk of teams working at cross purposes.

Response teams should include representatives from all areas of the organisation concerned with prioritised activities and those that support them, such as health and safety, facilities management, IT, etc. Top management should also be represented, as the decisions being taken may have a significant effect on the organisation. Although you do not need the entire top management team to be directly involved, the presence of one or more members will provide useful strategic direction and can help to legitimise difficult decisions, should they need to be made.

Team members with specific responsibilities during recovery should be assigned an 'alternate'. The alternate acts as a backup in case the primary team member is affected by the disruption or is unavailable for other reasons. Document the structure of the team and the roles and responsibilities of each team member so that the chain of command is clear to everyone involved in the recovery process. This document should also contain contact details for each member of the response team so that they can be easily contacted if a disruption occurs. Although not mandatory, this document should be maintained as documented information so that you can be sure that the correct version is in use (alternatively, include the responsibilities, contact information, etc. directly in the body of the BCP so all the information needed to use the plan is in one place).

The members of the response team should be competent to perform the roles and tasks expected of them. Specifically, the Standard requires the team members to be competent in a number of areas, including assessing the nature of the disruption and its possible impact, assessing the impact against your pre-defined thresholds and establishing recovery priorities (of which the first should always be the safety and well-being of employees and others for whom you are responsible). These competency requirements should be added to your competency matrix (see chapter 5) and monitored as part of your competency process.

Finally, you must develop documented procedures for each team that controls the "activation, operation, coordination and communication of the response".[14] This refers to the activation and convening of the team and its initial actions to discover the extent of the disruption (warning and communication, and specific response plans and procedures are covered in the next sections of the Standard), so you will need to develop procedures for activating your response structure, initial information gathering, how teams at different sites coordinate their actions and similar topics.

Information gathering can take a range of forms. Depending on the nature of the disruption, you may need to collect information from a multitude of sources: your departments, individual staff, suppliers and others. Very large organisations may need to collect information from multiple sites or countries, and even in different languages (which in turn may require translation if you do not have access to native speakers). The procedure should also describe how the information is recorded. All information collected during the initial response phase should be retained so you can evaluate the effectiveness of your response once the disruption is resolved.

Each of the procedures required by this part of the Standard relies on communication, so it is important to ensure that each procedure describes the communication methods to be used (and perhaps a backup method in case primary

---

[14] ISO 22301: 2019, 8.4.2.4b.

communications are disrupted). The procedures should be made available to the response teams in a format and manner that will not be affected by the potential disruptions you have identified (e.g. multiple storage locations, some in hard copy, some electronic).

8.4.3 Warning and communication

Without communication, even the best BCPs are doomed to failure. You must develop procedures that define "what, when, with whom, and how to communicate", bearing in mind that this includes both internal and external parties.[15] It may be beneficial to develop specific procedures for different types of communications: employees and emergency contacts in one, cross-organisation communications during a disruption in another, contact with emergency services in another, etc. You will also need a procedure that describes how you will document and record communications and how you will respond to those communications, especially those issued by national or local authorities.

Maintaining communications during a disruption can be a challenge. You must ensure that communication methods remain available despite the disruption, so that you can coordinate and manage your response. Although you may have considered alternative communication methods related to specific solutions earlier in the planning process, it is beneficial to develop this procedure in isolation, to better prepare the organisation for communication loss in scenarios where it is not anticipated. Communication resources should

---

[15] ISO 22301: 2019, 8.4.3.1a.

also be considered independently of any previously identified solutions for the same reason.

Interaction with emergency services will play a key role in many disruptions, and the Standard recognises this by mandating a procedure that facilitates "structured communication with emergency responders".[16] The procedure should define who is responsible for communication with emergency services (usually a mix of top management and department heads) and an alternate who can take over if the primary responsible person is unavailable.

You will also need a procedure that covers your organisation's media communications and response strategy. Disruptions of certain types (major hazardous spills, fires, floods, downtime of critical services, etc.) will inevitably attract media attention. Where the local strategy needs to align to a wider corporate or group media strategy, ensure that the high-level strategy accounts for business continuity factors to avoid potential conflicts during deployment, and as with emergency services, assign an alternate in case the person who is responsible for media communications becomes unavailable.

Item F in clause 8.4.3.1 requires that you develop a procedure that defines how you will record the details of the disruption and the actions and decisions taken in response. This could sensibly be combined with your information gathering procedure to create a single procedure whose output (e.g. an incident log) describes the disruption in detail,

---

[16] ISO 22301: 2019, 8.4.3.1d.

from initial investigation to the actions taken to respond to it, to the eventual recovery.

The last two items in this section are found in clause 8.4.3.2 and relate to alerting relevant interested parties that might be impacted by a disruption (whether actual or impending), and ensuring coordination where there are multiple responding organisations. This chiefly relates to man-made disruptions that have the potential to affect others or the surrounding environment, such as chemical spills, fires in premises that store flammable, explosive or nuclear materials, and any other scenario that might require you to inform neighbours, regulators or emergency services of potential hazards either in advance or when the disruption occurs.[17]

These two requirements only need to be considered 'where applicable', and if done properly, your risk assessment should already have identified scenarios that might be within their scope. If this is the case, consider how and when it might become necessary to inform interested parties and define how this will be done, what information will be provided, etc. Risk thresholds or criteria can help determine the risk level in a repeatable manner, and you will need to define the point at which information must be provided to ensure safety, the geographical areas that might be affected and other factors. You should also ensure that supporting procedures are functional and effective – safety data sheets and other information on potential hazards are up to date and available, and inventories carefully controlled and monitored

---

[17] UK organisations that store very large quantities of hazardous materials may have related obligations under the Control of Major Accident Hazards Regulations 2015.

so that emergency services know what quantities are stored (and where).

Coordination and communication between multiple responding organisations refers to scenarios in which your organisation and others (e.g. a neighbouring organisation) must respond jointly to a disruption – for example, if there is a risk of fire at your premises that could affect a neighbour, or vice versa. If applicable, you will need to meet with those who might be affected and agree on how you will communicate and coordinate, should the event occur.

The actions you each need to take will depend on the nature of the business continuity risk in question. The threshold at which joint efforts must commence, and the particular response actions and responsibilities (including alternates, where appropriate) for each party should be clearly defined, ideally in a written agreement. You may also wish to consider collaborating on business continuity exercises.

Note that warning and communication procedures must be included in the BCMS exercise programme to ensure they continue to function effectively over time.

8.4.4 BCP

BCPs are the culmination of all the work done up to this point. They are the core deliverable of the BCMS and a great deal of auditor attention will be focused on them. The Standard contains a long list of requirements that plans must comply with, so it is important to ensure that they are all met.

The requirements break down into two parts. The first part is as follows:

a) Details of the actions that the teams will take in order to:

    1) Continue or recover prioritized activities within predetermined time frames;

    2) Monitor the impact of the disruption and the organization's response to it;

b) Reference to the pre-defined threshold(s) and process for activating the response;

c) Procedures to enable the delivery of products and services at agreed capacity;

d) Details to manage the immediate consequences of a disruption giving due regard to:

    1) The welfare of individuals;

    2) The prevention of further loss or unavailability of prioritized activities;

    3) The impact on the environment.[18]

These requirements apply 'collectively' across all your BCPs, so it is not necessary for every single plan to include all these requirements. For example, you could reference the relevant activation threshold in each plan individually, or you could have a single document that describes all such thresholds and links to the plans that should be used if one is exceeded. Similarly, you could define how you monitor the impact of the disruption and your response in each individual plan, or in a separate document that outlines the monitoring approach for all the plans currently defined.

---

[18] ISO 22301: 2019, 8.4.4.2.

The second set of requirements apply to all individual plans. Each plan must include:

a) The purpose, scope and objectives;

b) The roles and responsibilities of the team that will implement the plan;

c) Actions to implement the solutions;

d) Supporting information needed to activate (including activation criteria), operate, coordinate and communicate the team's actions;

e) Internal and external interdependencies;

f) The resource requirements;

g) The reporting requirements;

h) A process for standing down.

Each plan shall be usable and available at the time and place which it is required.[19]

These requirements offer an outline of a well-constructed plan – defining what the plan does, who is responsible, how the tasks are performed, the supporting information and resources necessary to do it, and the reporting structure.

Although it may seem like a long list, remember that most of these requirements will be informed by the work you have done up to this point. Perhaps the only item on the list that has not already been considered is the process for standing down.

---

[19] ISO 22301: 2019, 8.4.4.3. Note that item a) refers to the purpose, scope and objective of the plan, not of the BCMS.

BCPs are not intended to operate over the long term. At some point, the organisation will need to stand down the measures it has taken to deal with a disruption and return to business as usual. It is important to note that the requirement to have "a process for standing down" refers specifically to the actions necessary to end the continuity measures defined in the plan rather than the measures taken to return to business as usual (the latter is covered later in this section).

The final requirement states that plans must be usable and available when they are required. Although this may seem painfully obvious, it is an aspect that is easily neglected over time, especially if the organisation operates multiple sites. Regular checks should be performed, regardless of the number of sites, to ensure that up-to-date plans are available for use where they will be needed.

The Standard requires that you "document and maintain" your BCPs but stops short of calling for them to be treated as documented information. Although the flexibility this provides is well intentioned, it is generally better to treat all documents that comprise your plans as documented information. Doing so allows you to ensure that the version in use is the latest available and provides a change history that can inform future development.

Developing BCPs

Developing BCPs can be challenging. There is a lot of information to juggle, and collating it all into a useful, easy-to-use format is time consuming, especially if you do not have a background in process design or technical writing, or a similarly appropriate field.

Each plan begins with a strategy – the broad strokes that outline how you will respond to a specific type of incident.

The strategy already defines how, when and why you will deploy the solutions it calls for (even if only at a very basic level), so all you need to do is take that information and expand upon it, adding enough detail and supporting information (while ensuring the above requirements are met) that the person responsible can pick up the plan and deploy it.

Many organisations opt for a pyramid structure for their BCPs. At the top, collective requirements such as activation thresholds, monitoring requirements, responsible persons, contact lists, etc. are defined for all plans within the BCMS. The layer below that comprises the plans themselves, covering all scenarios that pose a business continuity risk. The next layer down comprises the procedures, records, etc. that the plans rely on.

The relationship between the various component documents should be made explicit (e.g. via flow charts, links in the documents or simple text explanations) to avoid confusion, and to improve usability. Remember that there will often be long periods where the plans are not used, so it is essential that they are easy to understand and easy to put into practice (or at least, as much as is possible given the constraints of the scenario in question).

This approach provides a clear, simple structure to follow in the event of a disruption and lends itself well to visual representations that can be used to enhance training and awareness (posters, training slides, etc.) throughout the organisation. As the content of the plans themselves is compartmentalised, any changes identified over the lifetime of the BCMS need only be applied to a subset of the overall plan documentation – unlike more comprehensive, more 'vertical' plans, which would require the same change to be duplicated across multiple documents.

8.4.5 Recovery

Your BCPs will carry you through a disruption, but the temporary measures you put in place are not intended to become the new operating normal. To that end, the Standard requires that you develop documented procedures to restore your activities to business as usual once the disruption has been resolved.

'Restoring activities' refers to all activities, not just prioritised activities. Exactly what is required to return to business as usual will depend on the nature of your organisation, its facilities and the type of disruption experienced. It may be necessary to restore damaged premises, replace equipment, clean up environmental damage, etc. and you will need to ensure appropriate resources are available.

As with your continuity plans, there is benefit in ensuring a certain degree of flexibility in your recovery procedures. The order of activities necessary to return to business as usual will naturally vary depending on the type of disruption you experience, so overly rigid procedures may hinder rather than help the return to normality.

8.5 Exercise programme

For BCPs to be effective, they must be tested. To comply with the Standard, you must develop an exercise programme that tests your business continuity arrangements, so that you can evaluate them 'in action'. The results can then be used to make improvements.

The exercise programme must be based on "appropriate scenarios that are well planned with clearly defined aims and objectives", and must produce "formalized post-exercise reports that contain outcomes, recommendations and actions to implement improvements".[20] Your risk assessment has already highlighted the scenarios you might face, and you have already developed continuity plans to account for them, so the basis of your exercise programme already exists.

The next step is to develop the programme itself. You will need a schedule so that you can define the frequency and type of exercises and procedures that describe how exercises are conducted. The schedule should ensure that all scenarios for which continuity plans exist are tested over the course of a standard recertification cycle (three years).

The Standard also expects you to perform an exercise when there are "significant changes to the organisation or the context in which it operates".[21] Examples of such changes might include a move to different premises or buyout by another organisation. Changes of this scale generally take a long time to plan and implement, so there should be ample time to plan for a business continuity exercise to evaluate the new state of operations.

Conducting exercises

There is nothing in the Standard that defines how exercises should be conducted. Full-scale 'live' exercises are very valuable, but they require a lot of planning and resources to

---

[20] ISO 22301:2019, 8.5e.

[21] ISO 22301:2019, 8.5g.

ensure the best results and inevitably result in disruption to the organisation, so it is rarely feasible to conduct them on a frequent basis.

Instead of full-scale exercises, you can also conduct smaller-scale tests on specific procedures, or on parts of a BCP such as evacuation drills, initial reaction to and identification of a disruption, use of resources or any other easily isolatable aspect. You can also conduct tabletop exercises (discussions, question and answer sessions, verbal walk-throughs, etc.) to talk through how a plan will work and what problems might be encountered during use. Although not as comprehensive as a full-scale exercise, they can be performed more frequently and result in less disruption.

The ideal exercise programme makes use of both large- and small-scale tests. Plans and procedures deemed to be high risk or critical to recovery should be tested at scale and in their entirety, while lower risk and less critical plans or procedures can be tested in discrete parts to minimise disruption. Most organisations find that, as the BCMS matures and easily identified issues are resolved, larger exercises offer the greatest benefits, because they highlight issues that only occur when a plan is used in its entirety.

Procedures and review

Your exercise procedures should define not just how the exercise will be conducted, but also how the actions taken as part of an exercise differ from the actions taken in a real disruption. If you are testing a scenario involving fire, for example, you may choose to simulate a fire alarm rather than triggering the real thing. If you do opt to activate the real alarm, it may be necessary to inform the local fire service (and the owners of any adjacent premises) in advance. Any practical differences should be accounted for so that the test can proceed in as real a manner as possible, but without depleting resources acquired for recovery purposes or impacting other organisations or authorities.

The procedures should also define how information is gathered during an exercise (including who is responsible for doing so), and the output of the reports. Reports should contain outcomes, recommendations and improvement actions as required by 8.5e, and should also include information related to teamwork, competence, confidence and knowledge in line with 8.5c.

The Standard expects that you will implement changes and improvements based on the results of the exercise programme. Provided you can show how the issues identified in an exercise report are resolved – through updates to plans and procedures, resources, etc. – you should have no difficulty demonstrating improvement to an auditor.

8.6 Evaluation of business continuity documentation and capabilities

From time to time, you must evaluate your BCMS documentation in its entirety to ensure that it is effective and operating as intended. You must also conduct reviews after any disruption, and if significant changes to the organisation or its context occurs. The review must encompass your BIA, risk assessments, strategies, solutions, continuity plans and procedures, as well as the business continuity measures implemented by relevant suppliers and partner organisations.

The review should pull in all relevant data available on the performance and effectiveness of the BCMS: audit, exercise and post-incident reports, monitoring and measurement results, data on the competence of responsible employees, information on supplier business continuity measures, and information on legal requirements related to business continuity and how your organisation complies with them – along with any other information or data you deem useful.

The review is intended to evaluate the suitability and effectiveness of the BCMS, the organisation's compliance with legal requirements and best practice related to business continuity, and the organisation's compliance with its own business continuity policies and objectives. Although it is not explicitly called for, the review and its outputs should be documented to provide evidence that reviews are conducted, and to inform future reviews.

The Standard requires that any documents and procedures must be updated 'in a timely manner', implying urgency without describing a specific timescale. It is up to you to define what constitutes a 'timely manner', and it will be different for every organisation. For very large organisations, which must propagate changes across multiple documents at multiple sites and perhaps even in different languages, a timely manner might mean one or two months. For a smaller organisation operating out of a single site, a week or two might be reasonable, depending on the scale of the changes and the available resources. Delays occur in all organisations for a variety of reasons, so provided you can reasonably justify the time taken, you should not have a problem – however, bear in mind that disruptions can occur at any time and without warning, so leaving updates for too long can put your recovery capabilities at risk.

CHAPTER 9: PERFORMANCE EVALUATION

9.1 Monitoring, measurement, analysis and evaluation

All ISO management system standards include requirements for monitoring, measurement, analysis and evaluation of the management system. Monitoring and measurement play a key role in the continual improvement of the BCMS – if you do not know how the BCMS is performing, you cannot identify areas that could be improved.

The Standard allows the organisation to define the particulars of its measurement programme. You must decide what will be monitored or measured, the monitoring methods you will use, how often measurement or monitoring takes place, who is responsible, and how and when you will analyse and evaluate the results. When deciding what to measure, focus on things that are critical to the success of the BCMS, such as strategies, solutions and response procedures, and things that can provide information that can help improve the BCMS, such as resources used and the results of exercises.

You are expected to evaluate both the performance and the effectiveness of the BCMS. Monitoring performance demonstrates progress in the implementation of procedures, strategies, solutions, plans and other components of the BCMS – for example, the number of scenarios for which there is a defined BCP – while monitoring effectiveness demonstrates the impact of your business continuity measures, such as whether deploying a continuity plan results in recovery of the prioritised activity within its defined RTO.

In the early life of the BCMS, your measurements will likely skew towards performance, as you measure the progress of your implementation and identify areas that may have been missed in the initial set-up drive. As the BCMS matures, effectiveness measures become more useful, helping to identify areas where continuity plans and procedures are not providing the intended results. The 'ideal' measurement programme will use a mix of both performance and effectiveness, as appropriate for the current lifecycle stage of the BCMS, and will use both qualitative and quantitative measurements.

Under any management system, progress towards the system's objectives should always be measured, and a BCMS is no exception. You may also want to consider measuring performance during exercises, and the effectiveness of strategies and solutions, supplier business continuity measures and any other factor you deem relevant. Remember that the point of monitoring and measurement is to highlight areas where improvements can be made, so the first question when designing any measurement should be 'what will I learn from the data this will provide?'.

Analysis and evaluation

Monitoring and measurement produce data. To draw accurate conclusions from that data, you need to analyse and evaluate it in a consistent manner. The results of monitoring and measurement and the subsequent analysis and evaluation should be used to identify potential improvements to the BCMS.

You should define the methods used for analysis and evaluation in a documented procedure so that the same approach can be used across all your measurement data. The procedure should define the persons responsible and be linked to a schedule defining the type of measurement and the frequency at which measurements are taken.

Although not mandatory, it is beneficial to treat the procedure as documented information so that you can ensure the latest version is in use, and to provide a history of changes to the method so that historical data can be effectively compared to current or future data. It is, however, mandatory to maintain the *results* of monitoring, measurement, analysis, etc. as documented information.

9.2 Internal audit

Like monitoring and measurement, all ISO management systems include a requirement for an internal audit programme. Internal audits are intended to examine the BCMS and ensure that it meets the requirements of the Standard and the organisation's own requirements, and that it is implemented and maintained effectively.

Internal audits and those conducted by third-party auditors are fundamentally similar (though third-party audits are less frequent and more focused). The auditor examines an aspect of the BCMS and verifies that it conforms to the relevant requirement. If it does not, this is considered a nonconformity (nonconformities are discussed in more detail in chapter 10). The results of an audit are recorded in an audit report, which will describe areas of conformity and nonconformity, depending on what is discovered during the audit.

You will need to assign the role of auditor to a suitably experienced or trained person (or persons) within the organisation. If you do not already have trained auditors, you will need to hire someone with relevant experience or train existing members of staff.[22] Depending on the size of your organisation, you may only need one or two auditors, or an entire team or even multiple teams covering different sites. You can also outsource the role if necessary.

Auditors must be independent of whatever they are auditing, which means that internal auditors should never audit their own work. In smaller organisations where there is only one internal auditor, top management (with appropriate training or experience) often audit areas for which the internal auditor is directly responsible.

Audits must also be objective. Any evidence used during an audit should be factual – something the auditor has seen or heard directly – and be presented without bias. It is never appropriate to use second-hand evidence or information ("Bob said Katy does X", etc.) in an audit, except as a pointer to direct the auditor to areas of nonconformity that can then be investigated first hand.

Format and root cause analysis

Audits tend to use one of two formats:

1. Open ended; or
2. Checklists.

Audit checklists are useful because they provide structure and help newer auditors remember relevant requirements, but too much structure can inhibit the investigation process and lead to things that are not on the checklist being missed.

---

[22] IT Governance offers a range of training suitable for BCMS practitioners, including the Certified ISO 22301 BCMS Lead Auditor and Lead Implementer Training Courses: *www.itgovernance.co.uk/iso22301-courses*.

Open-ended audits involve no checklists, so they are reliant on an experienced auditor with strong knowledge of the Standard, but because they are not tied to a structure, they allow auditors much more freedom to 'follow' a nonconformity wherever it leads them.

Being an internal auditor is a little bit like being a detective. Although you may start out auditing, for example, the finance department, a conversation with members of the finance team might hint at a nonconformity in another area of the business. The auditor should complete the audit of the finance department, then investigate the possible nonconformity, wherever it leads them.

The 'detective' aspect also extends to root causes. All nonconformities identified during an audit should be investigated to determine the root cause. If an auditor determines, for example, that a BCP is not recovering a prioritised activity within the defined RTO, it is not enough to write an audit report that states 'Plan A does not comply with 8.4.4.2 a1'. Instead, the auditor should investigate further to determine the root cause of the problem.

Identifying root causes can take time and may require the auditor to follow a trail of issues to reach the 'core' of the problem at hand. If, in the example above, the RTO is not being met because the plan does not provide for enough resources, then not only is there a nonconformity in respect of providing enough resources to resolve, but the question also arises as to *why* the plan does not provide enough resources. If the answer is that the BIA process did not allocate enough, then the question becomes *why not?* – and so on, until no more questions can sensibly be asked and all the identified issues are resolved.

Audit reports

All audits should be recorded in an audit report. When writing audit reports, objective evidence is reported using neutral statements such as 'the auditor witnessed', 'the interviewee stated' and similar language. Reports should always reference the specific clause of the Standard (or the organisation's own requirements) against which a nonconformity has been identified, and the criteria and scope of the audit in question.

Some organisations opt to attach evidence of identified nonconformities to the audit report. Although this is a reasonable practice, physical evidence is not always readily available – for example, if a nonconformity is identified based on the statements of an interviewee, or through the auditor's direct observations (these are usually recorded as 'the interviewee stated Y'). If you do opt to attach evidence to audit reports, your audit procedure should recognise that doing so will not always be possible – in such cases, descriptions must suffice.

There is one other aspect of audit reports to consider: names. Although all audit reports should contain the names of key interviewees, some organisations link the names of employees to specific interview statements or nonconformities in audit reports, and some do not.

Employees are less likely to volunteer information if they believe (whether rightly or wrongly) that it may come back to haunt them. Audit reports are given to the manager of the department being audited as a matter of course (in line with clause 9.2.2 d), so naming employees who volunteer information – perhaps embarrassing the line manager in the process – can result in retaliation against the employee. In some cases, it can be better to redact names on the copy of the report provided to departmental managers to prevent this from occurring.

Although it is never pleasant to have to consider 'office politics', they are and will remain a reality in almost every organisation. Even one instance of retaliation, however small, can have significant repercussions on your audit programme – if employees feel that they cannot trust the auditor, or that telling the truth will get them into trouble (however 'unofficial' that trouble is), then they will not volunteer the information the organisation needs to properly maintain the BCMS.

9.2.2 Audit programme

The Standard expects you to develop an internal audit programme to structure your audits. The programme must define the frequency, methods, responsibilities, and planning and reporting requirements for internal audits. As such, the audit programme is often comprised of an audit schedule that defines the frequency, criteria and scope of each audit, and a supporting procedure that defines all other requirements. The schedule and procedure, along with all results produced by internal audits, must be treated as documented information.

Each audit should focus on a specific part or parts of the BCMS. The audit schedule should ensure that all aspects of the BCMS – including the internal audit programme itself – are audited. The frequency at which audits should be conducted is not discussed in the Standard, but you should consider it an unstated requirement that all parts of the BCMS are audited over the course of a year.

The programme must account for the importance of the procedures being audited, which means that it will be necessary to audit critical procedures, plans, etc. with greater frequency than less critical ones. It must also take into consideration any previous audit results, so an area or process that has been found to have nonconformities in previous audits should be audited more frequently to ensure that the nonconformities are resolved (and that no new ones arise). The increased audit frequency should be maintained until the area or procedure in question can demonstrate ongoing conformity.

The programme must define the criteria and scope for each audit. The scope defines the boundaries of the audit (e.g. 'the BIA process'), while the criteria define the requirements against which the audit is conducted (e.g. 'complies with ISO 22301 and the organisation's own requirements'). However, as noted earlier, the initial scope can and should be exceeded during root cause analysis or if the audit indicates a nonconformity in another area, so it is better to keep the scope (and to some extent, the criteria) as broad as possible so the auditor has some room to manoeuvre.

Corrective action

Nonconformities identified through internal audit must be resolved in a timely manner. Corrective actions should be issued through the nonconformity and corrective action procedure (described in more detail in chapter 10).

Corrective actions must be taken "without delay" and must also be followed up to verify that the action achieved what was intended.[23] The results of verification must be reported – you can align this to the reporting process in your audit procedure, or to the reporting process in your corrective action procedure, whichever is more appropriate. The

---

[23] ISO 22301:2019, 9.2.2f.

results, like all results produced by the audit programme, should be treated as documented information.

9.3 Management review

Another feature common to all ISO management systems is the management review. Top management must periodically examine the BCMS in detail to ensure it is achieving its goals and operating as intended.

It is up to the organisation to determine how frequently management reviews are needed, though it is common for them to be conducted on a quarterly, biannual or annual basis. Any longer period between reviews will probably be considered inadequate to ensure effective oversight of the BCMS and may be considered a nonconformity by a certification auditor.

The management review must include all the input requirements listed in 9.3.2. It is a long list, and some preparation will inevitably be necessary to collate all the information into a usable format. Because there is so much to cover, it may be beneficial to break up the review into multiple sessions rather than attempt to cover everything in a single meeting.

The review itself should examine the data provided to evaluate the BCMS and identify opportunities for improvement. Specifically, the review must output the requirements specified in 9.3.3: variations in BCMS scope and updates to the BIA, risk assessments, strategies, solutions and BCPs. This applies whether there are changes or updates necessary for the items in question or not – if changes are not required in some or all of these areas, the minutes of the review must reflect this.

The minutes of the review – or whatever method you are using to record the inputs, discussion, outputs and results of the review – must be maintained as documented information. The results of the review must also be communicated to relevant interested parties (e.g. employees). To avoid disclosing potentially sensitive information, you should review the results and redact or remove anything deemed confidential or privileged before release.

Where opportunities for improvement are identified, they should be recorded, implemented and reviewed after implementation to ensure they are effective. The easiest way to do this is to route improvement actions through the nonconformity and corrective action procedure (described in more detail in chapter 10). If you do opt to use a standalone procedure to track and control actions arising from management reviews, make sure that both it and the actions are treated as documented information, and that there is provision for reviewing actions after they have been implemented.

Although not mandated in the Standard, you should also consider conducting a management review after any disruption (regardless of whether plans were activated) and after any significant changes to the organisation or its context. This helps ensure that any major changes to the organisation are accounted for across all aspects of the BCMS.

CHAPTER 10: IMPROVEMENT

10.1 Nonconformity and corrective action

No management system always maintains 100% conformity. Over time, the various constituent parts of the BCMS will shift in and out of conformity as the organisation's operations evolve. This is a natural part of operating a management system, and the presence of nonconformities does not necessarily mean that the BCMS is failing to achieve its objectives – only that some aspects of the system are not operating as they should.

Nonconformities are usually grouped into three categories: major, minor and opportunity for improvement (often shortened to OFI):

1. **Major nonconformities** – indicate the complete absence of a requirement (e.g. no BIA process), prolonged or wilful failure to meet requirements or total failure of a component of the BCMS (e.g. an audit programme exists, but no audits have been carried out for six months).

2. **Minor nonconformities** – indicate requirements that are met in part, but that suffer from some non-critical deficiency that will not actively harm the operation of the BCMS (e.g. an out-of-date document was found to be in use, or a procedure is missing a mandatory requirement).

3. **Opportunities for improvement** – indicate minor deficiencies that do not currently pose a problem, but

that could become a problem in the future, and general improvement opportunities identified through the management review or over the course of normal, day-to-day operations.

These categories are used almost universally by certification bodies across the world, so although they are not defined in ISO 22301, adopting them will provide a useful link between your own internal nonconformities and those issued during certification or surveillance audits. Although there is nothing stopping you from developing and using your own classifications, bear in mind that confusion may arise if your classifications differ dramatically from those used by the certification body.

Corrective actions are exactly what they sound like: the actions you take to correct a problem. They can be a single action or a course of actions, and should be proportionate to the issue in question. Corrective actions are not always directly associated with a nonconformity – they can be issued independently if an opportunity for improvement is identified in the course of daily business.

The nonconformity and corrective action procedure

In a somewhat unusual move, the Standard does not mandate that you have a documented nonconformity and corrective action procedure (though it does require that you retain documented information on the nature of the nonconformities and the actions taken). Despite this, defining how nonconformities are classified and how corrective actions are issued, implemented and reviewed in a documented procedure (which should be treated as documented information) will ensure consistency and reproducibility, and is strongly recommended.

The procedure must begin by stating that where nonconformities are identified, the organisation will take action to control and correct them. It should then define the categories of nonconformity you will use (whether those listed above or your own) and how and where nonconformities will be recorded (e.g. in a spreadsheet or database). When recording nonconformities, it is important to maintain a clear link to associated corrective actions, so organisations usually assign each nonconformity a unique code or number that is also referenced on the corrective action form. This allows any corrective action to be traced back to a nonconformity, and vice versa.

The next section of the procedure must define how you evaluate the need to act in respect of any nonconformity to prevent recurrence. It must describe how you will review the nonconformity to determine if action is necessary, how you will determine root causes and how you determine if any similar or related nonconformities are present. As these are all investigative processes, your procedure should describe them in sufficiently broad terms to allow flexibility in their application.

This part of the procedure should also define how corrective actions will be issued, the format they will be issued in and who they will be issued to. The most common format is a corrective action form describing the nonconformity (and containing the unique reference code), the actions required to resolve it and with space to record a review of the action after it has been implemented.

Corrective actions

Corrective actions are usually issued to department heads or managers responsible for the business area in question, as they are responsible for ensuring that the action is implemented in a timely manner. Actions related to areas of the BCMS for which the business continuity manager or other persons involved in the operation of the BCMS are directly responsible, are usually issued to a relevant member of top management (on the understanding that the task itself may still be delegated), as top management retains ultimate responsibility for the operation and maintenance of the BCMS.

In some organisations, determining an appropriate corrective action for a given nonconformity is the responsibility of the auditor. In others, the action is determined by the department head or manager of the business area concerned, while still others require that the auditor collaborates with members of the department in question (not just managers) to determine the best course of action.

Of these, leaving it to the auditor or using a collaborative process between both parties is generally preferable. Allowing the department to define its own corrective actions in isolation risks ineffective or inappropriate corrective actions, inadequate reviews and is likely to generate conflict. The final decision as to whether a corrective action is suitable should always reside with the lead auditor, business continuity manager or equivalent role.

Implementation and review

ISO 22301 does not define timescales in which corrective actions should be implemented, and for good reason: it will be different for each action in each organisation. Some corrective actions cannot be implemented immediately, if for example they require resources with a long lead time or rely on other actions being completed first.

The question of timescales for corrective actions ultimately boils down to whether you can reasonably justify the time taken to implement the action in question. If a corrective action relies on equipment with a six-week lead time, it would be unreasonable to expect that action to be completed within two weeks of issuing the action. It would probably not be reasonable, however, to wait a further six weeks after the equipment has been delivered, unless there are other mitigating circumstances.

The importance of the action is also relevant – critical actions should naturally be prioritised over less critical ones. This is particularly relevant to the operation of a BCMS, as critical actions will usually relate to the organisation's business continuity strategies, plans and procedures on which recovery relies. A disruption can occur at any time without warning, so allowing critical corrective actions to go unimplemented, even for short periods, can seriously jeopardise the organisation's recovery efforts.

Corrective actions must also be reviewed to make sure they are effective. As with timescales for implementation, there is no set time frame for this and, for the most part, review frequency will depend on the action in question. Time must be allowed for the action to embed and for data to be gathered (where appropriate) to accurately determine effectiveness, so reviews are generally conducted anywhere from a week to several months after implementation.

You will need to show evidence of reviews to auditors, so it is sensible to leave space on the corrective action form to record the review (as suggested earlier). If the review indicates that the corrective action was not effective, then the root cause of the issue should be reviewed, further investigation performed as necessary and new corrective actions generated until the issue is resolved.

10.2 Continual improvement

Continual improvement is at the heart of all ISO management systems. You should always be looking for ways to improve the "suitability, adequacy and effectiveness" of the BCMS, based on the data you collect from monitoring and measurement, audits and any other relevant information.[24]

If you have implemented your BCMS in line with the Standard, then you already have continual improvement procedures: your monitoring and measurement programme, internal audit programme, nonconformity and corrective action procedure, and the management review. Clause 10.2 of the Standard requires that you use the data and analysis provided by these inputs to determine possible improvements to the BCMS and the organisation's operations.

It is up to you to decide whether it is necessary to develop a documented procedure for continual improvement. The Standard does not require one, and it is perfectly acceptable to point to the outcomes of the various input procedures as evidence of compliance with the requirement – no further action is necessary. If you feel that a documented procedure would benefit your organisation, however, then you should feel free to develop one.

---

[24] ISO 22301:2019, 10.2.

CHAPTER 11: ADDENDA

Certification

Despite publishing the ISO 22301:2019 standard, ISO is not responsible for certification. Instead, local certification bodies are accredited by national accreditation bodies to evaluate conformance and issue certificates.

In the UK, accredited certification schemes are managed by UKAS. In the US, the equivalent body is ANAB. However, it is important to note that there is no legal requirement for a certification body to be accredited. This creates a two-tier system of certification: those issued by accredited certification bodies and those issued by unaccredited certification bodies.

Accredited certification is valuable because the certification body has been independently assessed as competent to evaluate the management system in an impartial and objective manner. As a result, certificates issued by an accredited certification body will be recognised by suppliers, partners and other accreditation bodies across the world as a valid, independent determination of your compliance against the Standard.

Unaccredited certification offers no such confidence. Without independent verification of the certification body, organisations have no way to know whether the certification body is applying the standard correctly, so the certificate means very little. The absence of a logo from an accreditation body on the certificate will be an immediate red flag to anyone who examines it, and many organisations will reject it on sight.

If a customer or partner requests that you achieve certification to an ISO standard (no matter which one), they will almost invariably be referring to accredited certification. It would generally be unwise to secure certification from a 'certification body' that is not accredited by UKAS or by another national accreditation body. Similarly, if you need assurance from a supplier, you should check that any certification they provide is also from an accredited certification body.

The certification process

Certification is usually a two-stage process involving independent audits conducted by the external certification body.

The initial audit focuses on whether you are implementing the BCMS correctly and in line with the Standard, and will examine various key requirements to ensure they are being met. Do not worry if the auditor discovers nonconformities at this stage – this is common, and the auditor will use them as an opportunity to help you better understand the requirements of the Standard and how they should be applied.

After the first audit, you will have a clear idea of where you are meeting requirements and where you are falling short. You can then develop an action plan to implement any necessary changes to the fledgling BCMS in preparation for the certification audit.

The certification audit follows a similar process, in that it will examine the various constituent parts of the BCMS to ensure they comply with the Standard. The auditor will look for evidence that the BCMS is implemented, functional and operating effectively, which will likely involve reviewing evidence of audits, measurement analysis, management review, progress against objectives, etc.

The goal should be to begin the certification audit with confidence that there are no major nonconformities in the BCMS. Any minor issues noted can usually be resolved through your corrective action procedures, but any major nonconformities identified will likely result in the certification body refusing to issue certification until they are resolved to its satisfaction.

Maintaining certification

Once you have achieved certification, you then need to maintain it. Most accredited management system certificates are valid for three years, during which you will be subject to surveillance audits by the certification body.

Surveillance audits are usually conducted twice a year. Each audit examines different aspects of the management system (along with a subset of mandatory items that are included in all surveillance audits) so that the entire management system is independently reviewed by the time the certificate is due to expire. Members of top management should be present for surveillance audits, as they will be expected to be able to demonstrate knowledge of the BCMS and its objectives, adherence to the leadership requirements defined in clause 5.1 of the Standard and overall responsibility for the system.

Minor nonconformities identified during surveillance audits are generally left for the organisation to resolve on its own, though auditors will expect that the nonconformity is resolved and closed by the time of the next surveillance audit. Major nonconformities are usually resolved by developing and applying a corrective action plan that is agreed with the certification body.

If a management system is shown to be in conformity for extended periods (e.g. no nonconformities are identified for a whole three-year certification cycle), then the number of surveillance audits in future certification cycles may be reduced. Reducing the number of surveillance audits is entirely at the discretion of the certification body, however, and is never guaranteed.

Recertification

Towards the end of the certificate's lifespan, you will undergo a recertification audit. This will be similar to the certification audit and will examine your BCMS in detail, with additional focus on the effectiveness and performance of the system as implemented, the suitability of strategies, solutions, and objectives, and continual improvement. At the conclusion of the audit, the lead auditor will make a recommendation to the certification body in respect of your recertification.

Minor nonconformities identified during the recertification assessment are unlikely to affect the lead auditor's recommendation, unless they are present in large numbers or are indicative of a more significant problem. If any major nonconformities are identified, however, it is likely that the lead auditor will not recommend that your certification is renewed.

If this occurs, you will need to agree a corrective action plan with the certification body. This will describe how you will resolve the nonconformity and set a time frame within which another recertification audit must be conducted. If the nonconformity is not resolved, or the second recertification audit reveals further major nonconformities, then your certification will almost certainly be suspended or revoked.

The final decision always rests with the certification body. Most certification bodies permit the organisation to dispute the findings of a third-party auditor, but you should be very sure of your ground before making a complaint.

Business continuity manuals

If you are researching further information about ISO 22301 or undergoing training to learn how to implement or audit against the Standard, you may encounter something known as a 'business continuity manual'. This refers to a document or set of documents that act as a high-level guide to the BCMS, containing BCMS policies and objectives, the scope of the system, organisational charts and responsibilities, processes and process maps, and any other information deemed useful.

The concept of 'management system manuals' can be traced as far back as the 1994 edition of ISO 9001 (then ISO 9000-1), which mandated a 'quality manual' that described the scope of the quality management and contained key procedures and documentation. This requirement was subsequently included in all later editions of ISO 9001 until the release of the 2015 edition, when it was finally eliminated as a mandatory component (though many organisations chose to maintain their existing manuals for the sake of convenience).

After two decades of quality manuals, and as the increasing popularity of international standards resulted in many quality management practitioners expanding their skill sets to incorporate ISO 14001, ISO 27001, ISO 22301 and other popular standards, the 'management system manual' became ubiquitous, whether the standard in question mandated one or not.

11: Addenda

Of the two editions of ISO 22301 that have been released since ISO began publishing it, neither contains a requirement for a business continuity manual or anything resembling one. Duplicating key BCMS documentation in a 'manual' achieves little except to increase the amount of work needed to update and maintain its constituent parts, and those responsible for operating the BCMS and responding to incidents should, arguably, not require a manual or guide to assist them.

This is not to say that there is no benefit in having a 'single source of truth' that provides a concise, top-down view of the BCMS, but if you opt to implement one, it should function as an index – linking to the key documents rather than duplicating them and containing only the information necessary for that function. There is no need to create a 'manual' in the traditional sense.

FURTHER READING

IT Governance Publishing (ITGP) is the world's leading publisher for governance and compliance. Our industry-leading pocket guides, books, training resources and toolkits are written by real-world practitioners and thought leaders. They are used globally by audiences of all levels, from students to C-suite executives.

Our high-quality publications cover all IT governance, risk and compliance frameworks and are available in a range of formats. This ensures our customers can access the information they need in the way they need it.

Other resources you may find useful:

- *Disaster Recovery and Business Continuity – A quick guide for organisations and business managers* by Thejendra B.S, *www.itgovernancepublishing.co.uk/product/disaster-recovery-and-business-continuity*
- *Business Continuity and the Pandemic Threat - Potentially the biggest survival challenge facing organisations* by Robert A. Clark, *www.itgovernancepublishing.co.uk/product/business-continuity-and-the-pandemic-threat*
- *ISO 22301 BCMS Toolkit* by IT Governance Publishing, *www.itgovernance.co.uk/shop/product/iso-22301-bcms-toolkit*

For more information on ITGP and branded publishing services, and to view our full list of publications, visit *www.itgovernancepublishing.co.uk*.

To receive regular updates from ITGP, including information on new publications in your area(s) of interest, sign up for our newsletter at *www.itgovernancepublishing.co.uk/topic/newsletter*.

Branded publishing

Through our branded publishing service, you can customise ITGP publications with your company's branding.

Find out more at:
www.itgovernancepublishing.co.uk/topic/branded-publishing-services.

Related services

ITGP is part of GRC International Group, which offers a comprehensive range of complementary products and services to help organisations meet their objectives.

For a full range of resources on business continuity and ISO 22301 visit *www.itgovernance.co.uk/shop/category/bcm-and-iso-22301*.

Training services

The IT Governance training programme is built on our extensive practical experience designing and implementing management systems based on ISO standards, best practice and regulations.

Our courses help attendees develop practical skills and comply with contractual and regulatory requirements. They also support career development via recognised qualifications.

Learn more about our training courses in ISO 22301 and view the full course catalogue at *www.itgovernance.co.uk/training*.

Professional services and consultancy

We are a leading global consultancy of IT governance, risk management and compliance solutions. We advise businesses around the world on their most critical issues and present cost-saving and risk-reducing solutions based on international best practice and frameworks.

We offer a wide range of delivery methods to suit all budgets, timescales and preferred project approaches.

Find out how our consultancy services can help your organisation at *www.itgovernance.co.uk/consulting*.

Industry news

Want to stay up to date with the latest developments and resources in the IT governance and compliance market? Subscribe to our Weekly Round-up newsletter and we will send you mobile-friendly emails with fresh news and features about your preferred areas of interest, as well as unmissable offers and free resources to help you successfully start your projects. *www.itgovernance.co.uk/weekly-round-up*.